Real World
HUMAN RESOURCE STRATEGIES
That
WORK

Insight Publishing Company
Sevierville, Tennessee

Real World
HUMAN RESOURCE
STRATEGIES
That

Published by:
Insight Publishing Company
PO Box 4189
Sevierville, TN 37862

Printed in the United States of America

10 9 8 7 6 5 4 3 2

ISBN 1-932863-00-1

Table Of Contents

A Message From The Publisher

Some of my most rewarding experiences in business—or in my personal life, for that matter—have been at meetings, conventions or gatherings, after the formal events have concluded. Inevitably, small groups of ten to fifteen men and women gather together to rehash the happenings of the day and to exchange war stories, recently heard jokes or the latest gossip from their industry. It is in these informal gatherings where some of the best lessons can be learned.

Usually, in informal groups of professionals, there are those who clearly have lived through more battles and learned more lessons than others. These are the men and women who are really getting the job done, and everyone around the room knows it. When they comment on the topic of the moment, they don't just spout the latest hot theory or trend, and they don't ramble on and on without a relevant point. These battle-scarred warriors have lessons to share that everyone senses are just a little more real, more relevant and therefore, worthy of more attention.

These are the kind of people we have recruited for the *Power Learning* series of books. Each title offers contributions from men and women who are making a significant impact on their culture, in their field, and on their colleagues and clients. This edition offers a variety of themes in the area of human resource strategies. It is ripe with "the good stuff," as an old friend of mine used to always say. Inside these pages you'll find ideas, insights, strategies and philosophies that are working with real people, in real companies and under real circumstances.

It is our hope that you keep this book with you until you've dog-eared every chapter and made so many notes in the margins that you have trouble seeing the original words on the pages. There is treasure here. Enjoy digging!

Chapter One

HR Of The Future

Linda L. Bailey, SPHR

What will the human resources department of the future look like? How will it be different than what we experience today? We have all heard that the HR function of the future is going to be more strategic, and most of us agree with that prediction. But some of the questions we are asking ourselves are: "What does being strategic really mean?" "How are we going to know if we have successfully become a strategic Human Resource department, function or professional?" "What differences will being strategic make to our organization?"

The primary sources of measurement of a strategic function are its customer focus and client satisfaction. For HR, both external and internal customers will be measured. Internal customers are all employees, regardless of position. External customers include the purchasers of the business's product or service, stockholders and investors. To a lesser degree, external customers include vendors, suppliers, agencies and the communities in which organizations exist. Customer focus implies starting with the customer, external or internal, then thinking back to the organization and aligning the HR needs with the business needs.

In addition, programs, policies and practices will have a measurable effect on the bottom line. The CFO will become a collaborator

1

and ally. There won't be as many of us per employee head count, which is the old benchmark. Significant changes will occur in relationships with internal customers at all levels.

HR of the Future and the Employee

What does this strategic change in the workplace mean for employees? For one thing, they will continue to become more and more self-sufficient. The workplace will no longer be able to "take care" of its employees. Businesses can no longer afford to do so. The paternalistic organization can be very expensive. It also fosters an entitlement mentality. When employees expect a bonus or incentive simply because they were given one in the past, an entitlement mindset has crept into the organization. When employees complain about the size or amount of a gift, type of celebration or flavors of food, entitlement has permeated the organization. When organizations provide everything, employees stop thinking for themselves and for the organization. More effective and efficient processes and procedures will not be generated by non-thinking employees.

We've already seen the beginnings of what it means to be more self-sufficient in the arenas of health insurance and retirement plans. The workplace of the future realizes that these costs will need to be shared if the business is to stay viable. Learning how to be better consumers will become very important for employees. Health and wellness benefits and planning for a comfortable retirement are more and more becoming the employee's responsibility, and these new responsibilities will take some education. Providing this type of education will be the job of the employer. Most employees won't learn what they will need to know about insurance plans and retirement planning anywhere else.

The area of compensation is undergoing a major overhaul. Compensation systems are shifting from primarily a fixed-cost basis to variable-pay systems. That is potentially frightening for employees, especially those who are accustomed to receiving some type of annual increase based on years on the job. The transition to a variable-pay system needs to be well thought out and ideally introduced gradually.

Would you be willing to pay more for the car because it was made by employees who had worked at General Motors or Ford for fifteen years instead of five years?

Here's one example of how to communicate this change: When buying a car, would you be willing to pay more for the car because it was made by employees who had worked at General Motors or Ford for fifteen years instead of five years? The answer is obviously no. None of us would. This analogy can help employees realize that consumers are not willing to pay more for products simply because of a worker's seniority or longevity on the job.

Employees will have to get used to re-earning their wages every year, just like organizations do. Organizations cannot depend upon what they sold last month or last year; they have to continually provide current evidence of ongoing viability. Employees will likewise have to become comfortable with the same approach. They will have to become comfortable with part of their wages (and in some cases, all of their wages) being variable, based both on their performance and on how well the company does. If the compensation system is designed correctly, the portion of wages becoming variable will grow as employees become more comfortable with the new approach and realize that they can have a direct impact on their earnings. Annual merit increases are becoming a thing of the past. No business can afford $25-per-hour dishwashers. That can happen if employees are continually given raises year after year, without a review of the job's current value to the organization and to the marketplace. It's not to say that employees don't deserve some consideration for longevity; it just can't always be an increase in their base wages.

Employees can no longer depend upon the workplace to develop their career paths; they will need to take charge of their own career experiences.

Too many employees are more than willing to place their careers in the hands of their employers. That is a responsibility that employers can no longer exclusively accept. Employees can no longer depend upon the workplace to develop their career paths; they will need to take charge of their own career experiences. This includes more participation in the performance-appraisal process as well as career-interest tools and experiences. If employees are expected to contribute to the bottom line, they will want to know the direction in which the organization is going. The appraisal process will facilitate that knowledge by focusing on the present and future. The employee will have a responsibility to contribute to that process. The performance-appraisal process has been too one-sided in the past. The communication should flow both ways, becoming a fifty-fifty dialogue. Performance appraisals focusing on the past will become obsolete with variable-pay systems.

HR of the Future and the Supervisor

(For purposes of this discussion, "supervisor" refers to anyone who oversees employees, such as managers, directors, vice presidents, presidents, etc.)

Will the role of the supervisor change with regard to the HR function of the future? It already has in some organizations. The new, enhanced role of supervisors will involve more than just the bottom line. They will be measured on those "soft" items, such as turnover, employee complaints, absenteeism, accidents, etc. Their bonuses and raises will be affected by their success, or lack of success, in these and other HR-related areas. Companies should have a different performance-appraisal format for those who have supervisory responsibilities. Being an effective supervisor requires an entirely different set of skills than most generic appraisal forms outline. Some current managerial appraisals are the same as those for employees who don't have any supervisory responsibilities. And some organizations don't feel the need to appraise supervisors. As long as they're "on schedule and under budget," they are doing the job. In the information age, when intellectual assets walk out the door each night, being on schedule and under budget is no longer enough. The ability to provide an environment that makes employees want to contribute and grow takes additional skills—more than scheduling acumen and fiscal prowess.

Equally as important as recognizing and rewarding effective supervisory skills will be providing consequences for inappropriate behavior. Organizations are still rewarding for a successful bottom line only. But there is a lot more to it. In meeting the schedule, is there unnecessary turnover? Is valuable time being used in settling employee disputes? When job openings occur, can they be filled from within? Are there telltale absences on Mondays or Fridays? Do supervisors hire employees who can potentially take their (the supervisors') place, or are those hired not promotion material?

What does all this mean for existing supervisors? Some changes will be necessary. "Neanderthals," as some supervisors are known, will no longer be an affordable option in successful companies. One of the reasons is retention. We have all heard about and agree with the fact that it is easier to grow through existing customers than find new customers. The same principle can be applied to employees. The retention of key talent, which is defined as the ability to grow, find, move and develop key individuals in the organization, will become more critical than attracting new employees. And key talent will not work for Neanderthals for very long.

Additional training will not solve employee issues;
effective supervisory skills will.

The supervisor will no longer be able to pass his or her employee-relations issues on to HR. Supervisors will be required to deal with them on their own. HR will be there to train and coach, but they can no longer afford to be as hands on as they have been in the past. Supervisors will no longer be able to send employees back to HR, saying that they need more training, unless it is justified. Additional training is often used as an excuse for a lack of interest, motivation or execution. Additional training will not solve employee issues; effective supervisory skills will. In the past, those of us in HR have enabled this behavior; in the successful workplace of the future, we won't have the time, nor will we be perceived as very strategic if such enabling continues to be our focus.

Supervisors will play an important part in employee career development. Although employees will be taking greater charge of their careers, supervisors will have to provide the environment in which that can occur. This means that supervisors can no longer be threatened by hiring those who might be able to take their jobs or retaliate when hearing that their best employees are interested in moving on. It means that supervisors can't be fearful of sending their employees to off-site training and conventions because they might get recruited away. Too many supervisors do not support their employees in their desire to grow. And that leads to two results: 1) Employees quit (the controllable type of turnover talked about later) or 2) Employees mentally quit but physically stay (probably a worse scenario than the first).

What will the supervisor of the future need to know about HR? He or she will definitely need to know more about the "soft" aspects of HR. Supervisors will realize that employee-relations issues will need to be attended to on a regular basis, preferably daily. That means scheduling time in their calendars during the week for these activities instead of trying to fit them in at the beginning or end of the day. It could include jotting down points to be made in performance-appraisal meetings (which should occur more than once a year) and writing spontaneous personalized notes, when appropriate, about behaviors worth repeating. Many employees keep those notes for years—even though they may not be longer than two sentences—when they are specific and timely. Group "Atta boys" are okay, but praise and recognition mean more and are remembered longer when individualized. Supervisors could also get out of the office to do a little "management by walking around." They could talk with employees about something without a deadline or budget concern. This support of employee-relations activities is not going to happen without scheduling some time and giving it some thought. Listening and communication skills are also key.

HR of the Future and the Owner/President and Top Management

As the head of any organization sets the tone, top management might have some adjusting to do when it decides that the future organization will need to include strategic HR and employee focus to be successful. Not only is top management responsible for all that has been mentioned in the supervisory section above, it has some additional responsibilities.

Strategic planning is important, and involving as many as possible in the process will make it better. Mission statements, visions and values are extremely beneficial for all in the organization. It is very difficult to become a strategic HR department, function or professional without them. They can provide a great road map if they are authentic and believed and if they become part of the organization, not just an exercise.

Top management wants and needs results. By becoming more open-minded to the fact that the bottom line doesn't only represent dollars and cents, it might be surprised at the results it gets.

Top management wants and needs results. By becoming more open-minded to the fact that the bottom line doesn't only represent dollars and cents, it might be surprised at the results it gets. HR professionals have not done a very good job in the past of measuring the impact of turnover, absenteeism, accidents, tardiness, symptoms of bad morale, etc. on the bottom line. As those measurements become more accepted and used, top management will realize that those measurements can affect the bottom line, both positively and negatively. Providing the environment that allows employees and managers to grow, even if it means growing out of the organization, will be crucial. Providing an environment in which individuals feel appreciated, both personally and professionally, will produce the needed results. "Walking the talk" is crucial; being open-minded to those who point out when the talk is not walked is also crucial.

As the workforce becomes more self-sufficient, employees will expect their leaders to lead the way. There are at least two reasons for this. First, the old saying, "Never ask someone to do something you wouldn't do yourself" applies. Second, employees want to work for and with organizations they respect. When top management becomes greedy and self-serving, it will lose the employees' respect. Too many leaders say that their employees are their greatest assets without meaning it or knowing what it means. If that is the case, it is better left unsaid.

HR of the Future and the HR Professional

Besides continuing with our current responsibilities, what changes will be necessary for the HR professional in a strategic environment? We in the HR function will have to develop much more well-rounded business skills, including new financial acumen, starting with taking measurements and using numbers. It will include reading basic financial statements and knowing the jargon.

When beginning to take measurements and use numbers, please make sure they are useful. Some are not. Jay Jamerog, of the Human Resource Institute in Tampa, Florida, suggests asking, "Do they pass the 'So what?' test?" One statistic that doesn't pass the "So what?" test is the one stating how many employees have gone through training in the last year. Does the number of derrieres in seats (for training) tell us anything? No, I think not. The results of the training are what is important. What difference did it make? Did it improve productivity, reduce accidents, reduce complaints or improve customer satisfaction? When justifying existing training programs or looking for increases in budgets, HR professionals will have to get better at taking measurements and using numbers.

We will have to become better at hiring and promoting new supervisors. The skill sets we are talking about are not easy to interview for. Ensuring that a potential new supervisor has the skill sets to provide an environment where employees can contribute and grow, as well as positively impact the bottom line will become imperative. Sometimes we only question whether or not someone has supervised in the past. We have not made any effort to assess the effectiveness of their supervisory skills. In the future, the questions will focus on the effectiveness of their employee relation skills. Interview questions that probe into the "soft" skills will take some time and thought and should be developed in advance. Good supervisors can come in many shapes, sizes and styles. One test does not fit all. Good employee-relations skills are important, as is realizing that there is more to the bottom line than just the bottom line.

We are still promoting some for the wrong reasons—for example, elevating the best departmental employee to a supervisory role. We lose twice, if not more, that way. We lose the best employee in that position because we promote him or her, we usually lose some good employees because of the new supervisor's ineptness, and we experience a drop in productivity. HR will need to get much better at predicting who will be a good supervisor. Some individuals should remain individual contributors. Compensation systems will need to recognize this so that employees have choices and don't feel forced into supervisory roles. Some compensation systems only provide for growth for those who supervise others.

HR will need to get much better at predicting who will
be a good supervisor.

Compensation systems are already undergoing some significant changes. The movement from fixed-based systems to variable-based systems is well under way. The transition will be very difficult for some employees. Some experts in compensation allude to the fact it can be easier to start a company over than change an ingrained compensation system. Most employees find change uncomfortable, and changing the way they get paid will increase that discomfort to an unbelievable level. So include them in the planning.

Some HR professionals still mention cost-of-living adjustments. We will never be perceived as strategic if we are thinking about cost-of-living adjustments. Unless business is able to increase its price to customers every year because of the cost-of-living index, employees' wages certainly can't increase by it either. Employees will need to realize that only additional knowledge, skills and abilities will increase their value and, subsequently, their wages.

In looking at our appraisal processes, the tendency to think that our employees fall into a bell-shaped curve is misleading. Most of our employees are doing the jobs we hired, trained and are paying them to do most of the time. When inferring that they are in the middle of a bell-shaped curve, we infer that they are C-grade players. With the time and effort and money we spend to hire, pay and provide benefits for our employees, we are not purposefully hiring "C" players; we are hiring "A" players. Sometimes they do more than what we want, and sometimes they do less. But we are not purposefully hiring "C" players. Ask yourself this question: "When I go to have my oil changed, how many times do I expect the oil to be put back in?" or "When I have my hair trimmed, how many times do I expect it to be done professionally, the way I want?" The answer to both questions is, of course, every time. It is not unrealistic to expect our employees to perform the jobs we want 100 percent of the time. Perfect performance is not going to occur 100 percent of the time, but it certainly isn't going to occur only seventy percent of the time, which is what a bell shaped curve infers.

Some new thinking needs to take place in regard to some old programs. For example, why do we need performance appraisals? Why do we need job descriptions? Both have been around for a long time and need a serious overhaul. With all the changes we have seen, why haven't they changed much?

Some of the historical HR roles are diminishing. The first one that comes to mind is "the HR police." Compliance is still an important responsibility, but no one is going to perceive the HR function as adding value because COBRA is done correctly. Compliance is a basic expectation. Top management may need to be reminded regularly about the lack of legal fees, fines, etc. in these areas, because they are being handled efficiently and effectively. But because they have employed an HR professional, the expectation is that all those things are being managed. When HR is primarily perceived as the HR police, employees and supervisors will have a difficult time perceiving the HR function as an internal consultant since the skill sets appear to be incompatible.

With all these changes, HR professionals will need to become better facilitators. When asked to become more responsible for their insurance, retirement and careers while also putting their wages at risk, employees will want to be heard. Facilitating different methods for employees to be heard effectively will be important. What is done with the results will be more important.

Because of the need for employees to become more self-sufficient and take over responsibilities historically done by organizations, more education and training will need to occur in the area of retirement planning, health and wellness and career management. These are areas that employees have not felt any need to become knowledgeable of in the past.

And finally, we will have to enable less. Many in HR are enablers. We enjoy employees needing us. One example may be that we can't call the insurance companies for employees any more. However, we will have to make sure that we are selecting vendors who provide great customer service. One cannot go into this type of environment without the right partners.

One exception to enabling behavior may occur in small companies. Smaller companies, where the ratio of HR to employee head count is less relevant, may choose to maintain a culture involving some enabling. They may choose to continue to have HR do more hand holding. As long as the enabling choice is made consciously, knowing the pros and cons, and HR is perceived to be adding value doing that type of work, it may just work. But the challenge of minimizing the entitlement mentality will be more difficult.

Some HR professionals are not going to like the profession as much as it evolves into more of a strategic business partner. The old saying " Give a man a fish and you feed him for a day; teach a man to fish and you feed him for a lifetime" is particularly relevant now. We will need to start teaching employees how to fish. Some of us are going to miss feeling needed.

The Future Environment

This look at the future of external and internal HR environments is based on three assumptions, besides technological literacy. The first is that we are going to find ourselves in a tight labor market for the next number of years. The second is that the value of organizations is increasingly becoming more intangible (i.e. culture, competitive advantage, goodwill, etc.) as opposed to what is on the balance sheet. The third is that cost containment will continue to be a way of life. Since there are not many more ways to contain costs and demands are still increasing, improvements will have to occur a different way.

Summary

Who will find the upcoming challenges the most daunting? Certainly, some individual members of each group will not enjoy the new and different future. But most will. Those employees who are sure of themselves and their skill sets will look forward to being paid according to their value and contribution. Those managers who adapt and effectively demonstrate the soft skills will be amazed by how much their employees can contribute. Those in top management who are willing to be open-minded and realize that the bottom line is not just the bottom line will get the results they want and need. And those in HR will find their profession much more gratifying by adding value that is measurable and recognizable. It is a great time to be in HR. What we do now can really make difference, both to the bottom line and to all parties involved.

About The Author

Linda L. Bailey, SPHR

With over twenty years of experience as a Human Resources generalist, Linda Bailey, SPHR, is a consultant, speaker, trainer and teacher on many Human Resource issues while emphasizing the employer-employee relationship. With a goal of "helping employers from needing employment lawyers," her expertise covers both crises intervention and continuing management solutions. Linda has worked with organizations in many capacities; from coaching them through difficult employee decisions to developing and presenting customized workshops for those that have supervisory responsibilities. Workshops cover the entire employment relationship, from hiring to firing, with the most popular workshop request being harassment awareness. Customized consulting services are based on each organization's human resources needs. Linda majored in Psychology at the University of Wisconsin and graduated with a Bachelor of Arts in Business Administration from the University of South Florida. Her corporate experience has occurred in various industries, with a Fortune 300 company, and as a Vice President of Human Resources for a PEO, (a professional employer organization). As a member of the Society of Human Resource Management (SHRM) since 1979, she holds their highest certification, the Senior Professional in Human Resources (SPHR). She is also a member of the National Speakers Association, and its local chapter. As a member of the teaching faculty of the Division of Professional and Workforce Development at the University of South Florida, she teaches a number of courses in the Human Resources field.

Linda Bailey, SPHR
Bailey Consulting Group
10460 Roosevelt Blvd, #234
St. Petersburg, Florida 33716
(727) 528-0556
Linda@BaileyCG.com
www.BaileyCG.com

Chapter Two

Seven Keys To Extraordinarily Effective Interviewing And Making Great Hiring Decisions

James M. Vance, PE, SPHR

Effective staffing is the lifeblood of any organization. Productivity, profitability and the degree to which a work environment is agreeable depend on it. When the staffing component of business is handled well, turnover and internal conflict are reduced, and job satisfaction and the relative contribution an employee makes is increased.

Effectively staffing any organization begins with the interview process. Using explanation and example, this chapter will walk you through seven keys to conducting extraordinarily effective interviews and making your hiring effort successful.

Seven Keys to an Effective Interview and Hiring Success

1. Work to support a long-term staffing solution.
2. Build a conscious relationship.
3. Clearly and realistically define the What of Fit.
4. Clearly and realistically define the How of Fit.
5. Formulate the right questions.
6. Use techniques that make it easy for a candidate to tell you what you need to know.
7. Tap into hidden communication.

1. Work to Support a Long-Term Staffing Solution

We will begin our discussion by looking at establishing a *long-term staffing solution*. Keeping a longer-term perspective is the first key to the interview process. A long-term staffing solution goes beyond a short-term outlook (which focuses on immediately filling an internal need) and focuses on a bigger picture.

A long-term staffing solution goes beyond a short-term outlook (which focuses on immediately filling an internal need) and focuses on a bigger picture.

This bigger picture takes into account the factors that make an employee want to stay with your organization, and it considers the consequences of hiring someone who does not fit in with your organization.

There are many costs associated with a hiring mistake in your business. Direct costs include the administrative expense needed to get an employee into and out of your pay and benefit system, training hours expended on the employee, productivity losses, time and expense needed to terminate the employer-employee relationship and resources expended to find a replacement. There are also hidden costs. These indirect costs include:

The personal cost of the hiring mistake

The personal hurt and lowered self esteem that come from an employee-job role mismatch affects all of us. In fact, it affects the fabric of society at large as our families, friends and loved ones deal with the healing of these emotional wounds. In extreme cases, the cost to your company could be the grievous consequences of workplace violence perpetrated by departing employees who use unresourceful means to reconcile the hurt.

Costs due to the loss of a sense of competence in the workforce

Competence breeds confidence. When employees lose faith in themselves or in the organization, there is a negative impact on productivity.

Cost to the company's reputation

If your employees or the departing employee feel that an injustice has been done, there will be a negative hit to your company's reputation.

A long-term staffing solution takes these costs into consideration. It also embraces a strategy through which hiring mistakes and their associated costs can be minimized. Applying this strategy means approaching the staffing process with an awareness of what the employer and employee need from the work relationship. It also means approaching the staffing process with the following success principles of motivation and conflict resolution in mind.

Human Motivation and the Long-Term Staffing Solution

Effective motivation goes far beyond carrot-and-stick methods. It borrows concepts from current motivational theory, successful mediation efforts and best practices of employers with high levels of employee commitment. For the purposes of this chapter, we will provide working principles from each area, explore how they overlap and apply these lessons to the business interview.

It is easy to demotivate an employee. A manager simply needs to ensure that an employee doesn't know what he is supposed to be doing and provide little or no favorable feedback to the employee. (The potency of this demotivating approach can be increased by ensuring that negative feedback is provided.)

The colloquial term for this is "mushroom management": People are kept in the dark and covered with fertilizer. Common sense confirms mushroom management's demotivating effects, but current motivation theory provides an antidote to its poison. Current motivation theory tells us that for sustained motivation, the following are needed:

- Clear goals that are meaningful to the employee
- Clear rules for participation
- Evidence of meaningful progress
- Challenge that stretches the employee near the edge of his ability
- Positive feedback (letting an employee know what he is doing well)
- Opportunity to use skills in more complex work situations

These motivational lessons dovetail with the results of studies of organizations with high levels of employee commitment and those that are succeeding in troubled industries. These studies show that such organizations share the following characteristics:

- There is open communication.
- A sense of common interest has been established.
- The importance of relationships is acknowledged.
- Management is reliable, helpful and responsive.
- Management tells the truth and admits mistakes.
- There is a sense of fairness.
- Both management and employees are objectively held accountable.

If you look closely at the characteristics of high-commitment organizations, you will find that they restate our understanding of motivational factors in a different way. A "high level of employee commitment" is another way of saying that an organization has a motivated workforce. "Management reliability" is another way of saying that there are clear rules for participation in the workplace.

Managing Conflict and the Long-Term Staffing Solution

It is worth noting that these high-commitment organizations are not free of conflict; they simply handle conflict constructively. They use the same principles used by mediation specialists.

These specialists tell us that conflict ends when conflicting parties see a mutual benefit in working together that is of greater value than the perceived benefit of not working together. High-commitment organizations use conflict-resolution processes to work toward greater interpersonal understanding and acknowledgment of the mutual benefit of working together. They work to understand the needs of both parties and to foster the recognition that fulfilling those needs is in their mutual best interest.

A fair environment is one in which an individual is treated with dignity. This means that an employee is invited to use talents and abilities to contribute, rather than be confined to a role that limits or denies such involvement. In the ideal environment, a person is challenged near the edge of his abilities and is given the feedback and support that indicate progress and lead to success.

In the ideal environment, a person is challenged near the edge of his abilities and is given the feedback and support that indicate progress and lead to success.

As a potential employer, you are more likely to hire people who are committed and motivated if these principles are kept in mind. This means bringing the long-term solution to the interview process and consciously working to build a strong employer-employee relationship.

2. Build a Conscious Relationship.

The second key to the interview process is to build a conscious employer-employee relationship. This goes beyond "Can he or she do the job for us?" It means specifying the needs of the employer. It also means using the interview process to understand the needs/goals of a prospective employee.

Look at the following chart.

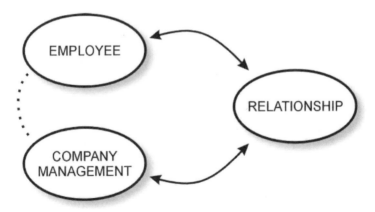

This chart tells us several things about conscious relationships.

1. The relationship is an independent entity that exists separately from either party. It has no physical presence, existing only in the minds of both parties.

2. If the relationship were to go away, both parties would remain intact. Ideally, neither party views the relationship as more important than its own needs, although, as in any long-term relationship, each must be willing to give in to the greater good of the relationship. To preserve the long-term benefits of the relationship, short-term compromise is occasionally needed.

3. The relationship becomes a vehicle to fulfill the needs of each party. The conscious relationship exists only to the extent that each party understands what it needs from the other and behaves accordingly. Figuratively, the relationship is a goose that lays the golden eggs of need/goal fulfillment. Both parties must behave in a way that maintains the long-term health of the goose.

4. Finally, it depicts the opposite of the more common, unconscious scenario. When a relationship is started without conscious intent, both parties enter the relationship with unspoken assumptions as to what the relationship should be. They enter into the relationship believing that the other party will automatically agree to these unstated assumptions. The seeds for conflict and turnover are sown.

This unconscious scenario will be explored in the following real-life example.

Let's say that you run a staff of ten and need to hire an administrative assistant. Let's assume further that your workplace is growing and that few internal systems are in place. The demands of your workplace mean constantly shifting priorities. You talk with a potential hire, and you like the person. He has a professional presence, excellent writing skills and has managed filing for a much larger, more established organization. You hire this person, thinking he can use his large-organization experience to improve your smaller organization.

Suppose that you require ten-hour days and occasional overtime as well as quick thinking on the fly. You are busy and want your hire to figure out what to do with minimal input from you. You want flexible systems set up that can adapt to the changing needs of the organization.

Let's assume that the person you have just hired is very good at maintaining existing systems and duplicating what was done at his previous company. He wants no more than a forty-five-hour work week, and holidays are important to him. He is very uncomfortable creating a new system and requires your approval and feedback for each step, no matter how small.

If you are like many hiring managers, your interview process will not have uncovered the mismatch. To uncover it, the interview process must look at both the What and How of Fit. The process must look at the skills, knowledge base and experience necessary for success on the job. It must also look at the preferred approaches to work that will be needed for success.

3. Defining the What of Fit.

The third key to the interview process is to define the What of Fit. Let's continue with our administrative assistant scenario. The likely outcome of the situation that was just described is a frustrated manager. This frustration will probably result in the departure of a frustrated employee who feels like he is a square peg being forced into a round hole. On the other hand, the hiring manager will probably think he has come face to face with someone who just didn't get it. The scenario can be explained using the following chart, which depicts the What of Fit.

Chart 1

Commitment Versus Tenure in an Employer-Employee Relationship

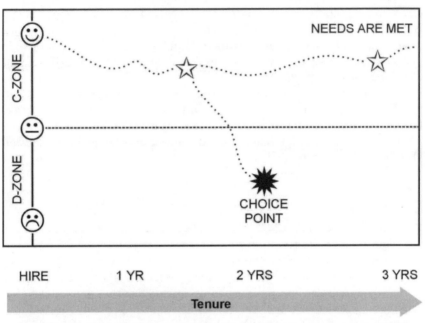

C-Zone = Commitment Zone   D-Zone = Departure Zone

The reality of the workplace is that most employees enter the relationship without clearly defining their needs. These needs revolve around the issues of security, belonging, achievement, status and accomplishment. They translate into job stability, pay and benefits, time with family, time to pursue outside interests, favorable peer relations, favorable management relations, valuable new experience, promotion, title, accomplishment and successful utilization of talent. These are the goals of the employee. Your needs will also cluster around the same issues but will translate into honesty, relative harmony of work relationships, productivity, profitability and perpetuation of the business model. These are your goals.

When a company works to understand the needs of an employee and communicate the organization's needs, it goes a long way toward acknowledging the importance of the relationship. The chart shows us that:

- To the extent that both parties feel that they are in the process of meeting their respective needs and goals, there is commitment.

- To the extent that either party receives internal or external feedback that makes it question whether its needs are being met by the relationship, the relationship is at a choice point. This is the point at which the parties can choose to communicate and explore whether there is a mutual benefit of working together that is of greater value than the cost of departure. The parties can also choose to do nothing and end the relationship. It is worth noting that many relationships experience an emotional end rather than a physical end. Simply putting in time and an uninspired workforce are its symptoms.

The What of Fit—An Example

The third key to the interview process takes shape in a brainstorming session attended by the hiring manager, a representative from HR and, if appropriate, individuals who will interact closely with the new hire.

The brainstorming session develops specifications for the interview process. This session takes a hard look at the answers to three focused discussions. These are:

- What experience, knowledge, skills, qualities and characteristics are needed for a person to be successful in this role?

- What qualities and characteristics would cause a person in this role to fail?

- What does the company realistically offer the employee in an employer-employee relationship?

Let's explore how such a brainstorming session might work. Let's imagine that the administrative assistant will report to a department head and have to work closely with people at all levels. Let's say that your company is in the construction business. As a human resource

- The opportunity to get involved with new things
- Average pay to start; above-average increases for performance
- Long hours but family friendly
- Slower periods during bad weather and Christmas season
- Loyalty to office staff
- Projected additional opportunity due to growth.

The Lists Become a Template for the Interview

The three lists form a more realistic description of what you need and can provide to an employee. These lists become the first of two templates for an effective interview. These lists should be used to measure the *What of Fit*. They should be used to shape the interview.

The first template, while important, is incomplete. It looks at what an individual has done as an indicator of future performance. It fails to look at approaches to work that must be used to succeed in a role. A second organizing step is needed prior to taking action. A second template based on preferred approaches to work must be developed. You must work with the hiring manager to map this out. In doing so, you determine the *How of Fit*.

4. Determining the How of Fit

Employment laws can penalize a company financially when it makes distinctions based on race, color, gender, religion, national origin, age, citizenship or disability. Essentially, these laws require today's employer to provide a workplace that is perceived as fair. Interviews should make distinctions based on legitimate business needs as well as knowledge, education, experience and ability necessary to perform the tasks of a job. They should make distinctions based on ability to do the job and ensure that a company hires the most qualified candidates. By making decisions in this manner, we reduce the risk of legal issues.

There is, however, a hidden source of discrimination in the workplace, one that exists beneath the surface of any organization and is not considered by employment laws. It is not illegal, but practicing it can be costly. It is the belief that others should naturally use the same approach for completing a given task that we would. This assumption is often far from the truth. Failure to understand this can leave a hapless hiring manager trying to teach a cat to swim, when he would have been better off hiring a fish.

Consider the possibility that you might interview two equally qualified candidates based on the first template that we just developed. If your interview focused solely on background, would it uncover the following?

1. One candidate is very uncomfortable in an unstructured environment and is thrown for a loop if there are no established guidelines. This candidate likes to stick with a task until it is finished. Working within a system, he is very good at maintaining it.

2. The other candidate is good at solving problems that she has never faced before. This candidate has successfully worked to improve every system of which she has been a part.

Within this scenario, it should be obvious that if your hiring manager likes to do things his way and doesn't handle suggestions from new employees well, one candidate will be better for the job than the other. By the same token, if your hiring manager encourages system improvement and seeks employee input, then the other candidate would be a better pick.

There are a number of issues that can crop up if situations like this are not considered. Each and every position has its own breakdown of the relative importance of:

- adherence to standards
- facility with written or spoken language
- comfort level with risk and issues
- interest in detailed involvement
- hands-on work in the physical world
- problem solving.

Furthermore, in each position, there will be the need to either establish new systems and modify existing ones, or maintain existing systems. Let's consider the example of the administrative assistant further. For ease of understanding, the following matrix can be used as a guide.

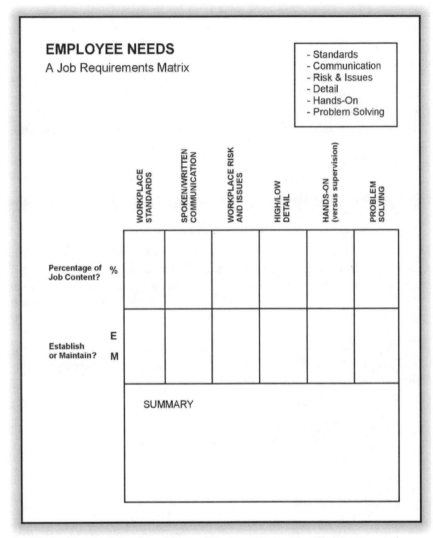

The matrix is designed to focus your thoughts on how the job must be done in order for the person to be successful. Breaking down the role into requirements for how the job should be done is the fourth key to the interview. This process forms a second template that can be used to give the interview a final focus.

In our construction company scenario, let's assume that:

- five percent of the job will be maintaining existing standards
- twenty-five percent of the job will involve using spoken and written communication
- fifteen percent of the job will call for untried solutions in an unstructured environment
- ten percent of the job will be high-detail proposal writing and data keeping
- five percent of the job will be hands-on filing
- forty percent of the job will require problem solving and coming up with realistic solutions

For this scenario, there is limited maintenance of existing systems. Most of the work will involve the establishment of some type of order in your unstructured environment. It is important to note that there are people who will naturally fit into this position, and there are those who will not. If you hire someone who isn't a close match in these areas, you will wind up with someone who does not fit the role. Once this second template is worked out for the position, you are ready to begin the next step of the interview process.

5. Formulating the Right Questions

To get the most out of the interview, make sure that questions are open ended and that the interview is structured around the following pattern:

	WELCOME CANDIDATE	
SELL COMPANY AND OUTLINE NEXT STEP	ASK APPROPRIATE QUESTIONS GEARED TO PERFORMANCE OF JOB	DESCRIBE INTERVIEW PROCESS
	LET CANDIDATE ASK QUESTIONS NEAR END OF INTERVIEW	

The questions you actually ask should arise naturally from the two templates. Using the templates that we built for the administrative assistant position, you might generate the following questions:

- Tell me about your administrative experience.
- Describe a typical day on your previous job.
- Why do you want to leave?

- If your ideal job fell in your lap, what would it be like?
- How is the workplace different because you were there?
- Suppose you were to come into an environment with ten people and very limited filing and record-keeping systems in place. How would you approach the job?
- Please share with me what the personalities were like on your past job. Who did you enjoy working for and why?
- If you could restructure your day to best suit the way you like to work, how would you make it different?

Once you have come up with core questions that stand a good chance of unmasking whether the candidate is a match based on the two templates, you are ready for the next step in the interview—talking with the candidate and making conversation flow.

6. Make Conversation Flow

The sixth key to the interview is to use a structure that facilitates the flow of conversation. This means making it easy and comfortable for the candidate to tell you what you need to know. The way to do this is to pre-frame the interview, ask open-ended questions, periodically compliment the person and ask questions using words that the candidate has already used. This is what talk show hosts do when they are conducting a non-confrontational interview. Try it; you will find that it works!

To make conversation flow, begin by pre-framing the interview. This means telling a candidate what to expect and defusing some of the fear that most people feel when in an interview.

Example:

Interviewer: Hi, Mary. Thank you for coming by. I'm Jane Jones, and I want to tell you how our interview process will work. After you've filled out an application, I will come and get you, and we will talk for fifteen to twenty minutes. Then I will have you meet with our hiring manager. Our people are pretty busy today, but if we can get people to break free, we may have you meet with one or two other people. (This language gives you the option of cutting the interview short if it becomes obvious that the person is unqualified or is not a fit.)

31

they promoted me into the position. I've been working in that role ever since.

Interviewer: You were promoted after only six months. That's impressive. Will you share with me why you were promoted?

Answer: There was an opening, and they thought I could handle it.

Interviewer: And why did they think you could handle it?

Answer: When I got there, there was a system in place that was not being used. The company was spending a lot of time trying to locate records. I went to a class and figured out how to use the system. After just a couple of months, the company had stopped having its problems with record location.

(As Mary answers the question, you notice that she has slumped slightly in her chair and is less than enthusiastic about her accomplishment.)

Interviewer: Mary, I sense that there is a little more to it than that. You mentioned that it took a couple of months. Can you tell me more about that?

Answer: I went to my boss and told him what I thought needed to be done. He told me to go ahead. I sent out a memo to everyone in the office telling them about the new system. At first people ignored it, so I made out procedures for everyone.

Interviewer: That seems like a logical approach. How were the procedures received?

(Prolonged silence as Mary seems more uncomfortable.)

Interviewer: It's okay to tell me. I'm just trying to make sure that we've got a work environment that you can thrive in.

Answer: People got upset about having to change the way they did things. People gave me a hard time about the change.

(You notice that her body posture continues to slump slightly.)

Interviewer: What happened next?

Answer: My boss called a meeting and told everyone that I was doing what he'd asked me to do. He told them that for the good of the company, they had to adopt the new procedures and that if they had any issues, to come to him. After that, things quieted down. Once people saw the new system working for them, they were okay.

Interviewer: Change can be difficult for anyone to implement. It sounds like even though people gave you a hard time, it worked out okay. (Mary nods in agreement.) Tell me, Mary—if you had the choice of being put in a similar situation again or being put in a situation where the systems were already in place and working well, which would you choose?

Answer: One where the systems are already in place.

In this brief example, it is plain that Mary is not a fit for your role. Working in an unstructured environment is not her preference. Furthermore, you need someone who will quickly improve your systems. People who are good at initiating change do not lose heart at the first sign of resistance. In most cases, taking the next few moments to spell out what the job really needs (the How of Fit) and asking Mary if she wants to continue to pursue the opportunity will convince her that she does not want the job. By tapping into hidden communication as you explore this issue, you may even find that she is grateful for your approach to the interview and more than happy to cut it short. You can save time and quickly get on to the work of finding the right person for the role.

Putting It All Together

No one wants to be put in a role where they will not succeed. No employer wants to hire someone who does not work out. It's costly on both sides. Avoiding this cost begins by entering into the interview process with conscious intent and a long-term picture in mind. By structuring your interview process so that you clearly and realistically know what you want, you can streamline the hiring effort. By defining what you offer an employee in the employer-employee relationship, you help avoid unrealistic self-opinion. You work to avoid hiring someone who comes on board with unrealistic expectations. By focusing on the What of Fit and the How of Fit, you work to hire people who will be both motivated and committed to your organization and the role you have for them. Formulating questions that stem from the What and How templates and tapping into hidden information help candidates tell you what you need to know honestly and forthrightly. By putting the Seven Keys to an Effective Interview and Hiring Success into action, you are on you way to conducting extraordinarily effective interviews and making great hiring decisions.

About The Author

James M. Vance

Jim Vance, PE, SPHR is president of Advanced Business Resources (ABR), a firm that specializes in people management and communication training. A former HR and Training Director, and seminar leader on the national circuit, Vance has spoken to business audiences in thirty-eight states. He has managed staffing efforts for all position levels, and has led recruitment for enterprise resource planning initiatives. Vance regularly presents many business programs including *The Layperson's Short Course on Applied Personnel Law, Understanding the Process of Effective HR Practice, Conversational Interviewing ™, Emotional Intelligence: Useful Tools for the HR Practitioner,* and *Relationship Management for the HR Business Partner.* Known as a true teacher who engages his audiences from start to finish, Vance's keynotes and seminars provide useful information that has immediate real world application. Information regarding delivery of an ABR program at your place of business can be found on the Advanced Business Resources web site, www.abr-training.com.

James M. Vance, PE, SPHR
President
Advanced Business Resources
4912 Yoakum Blvd.
Houston, TX 77006
713.527.8893
hrstrategies@abr-training.com
www.abr-training.com

Chapter Three

Human Resources, Heal Thyself: Leading Human Resources In Uncharted Territory

Brenda L. Johnson, SPHR

In the 1990s, business struggled to cope with technology, a multi-generational workforce and globalization. The new millennium heightened those concerns and added new ones, including bioterrorism, corporate ethics crises and a sluggish economy. Business leaders counted on human resources professionals to help them work through the impact these new realities had on the workforce. Human resource professionals were often charged with coordinating workforce reductions affecting thousands of employees and addressing concerns of workers about the dwindling balance of their retirement accounts. While all of this was happening, the profession was going through a transformation of its own. Today, the field of human resources continues to evolve, and business leaders continue to ask more of human resources professionals. During this time of transition, human resource leaders also must ensure that professionals in the field have the support, technology and training to lead business through continued uncertainty.

From Administrative Cop to Strategic Partner

Compliance with the dictums of human resources was once forced by government regulations. The personnel department was an administrative function, ruling with the power that came from acts of Congress like ERISA and COBRA. The power of personnel was unquestioned since it was responsible for policing any noncompliance that might result in a financial or legal risk to a business. Personnel was responsible for the oversight of employee benefits as well as compliance with regulations and laws concerning workers, and it worked with union leaders to ensure compliance with labor contracts as the workforce moved from an agriculturally-based economy into a manufacturing-based economy. The workforce was primarily Caucasian, male, and careers ended with retirement after spending a significant period with a single employer.

The Baby Boomers, born between 1943 and 1960, came into the workforce with a different attitude than previous generations. The economy also slowly changed from an intense manufacturing model to more of a knowledge-based framework, and women began entering the workforce. Over time, human resources' role moved from policing and administration to proving value by partnering with management. In the '80s, it was common for human resources to want a "seat at the table" where business decisions were being made to proactively consider the workforce. Moving from policing and administration to partnering as part of the management team has continued to prove a difficult transition in some organizations.

As the economy moved further into a knowledge-based framework and became more information driven, organizations began to re-evaluate their missions and strategies. To remain competitive, most successful organizations adopted a customer-centered strategy. This required business leaders to partner with human resources in designing and developing the organizational capabilities needed to help the workforce remain competitive. During the '90s, organizations like Southwest Airlines and Nordstrom became known for their employees' focus on the customer. The business media highlighted stories of a workforce able to do a superior job of implementing customer-driven strategies. Business magazines like *Fast Company* and *Business 2.0* made heroes of organizations with workers who could meet the demands of information-laden customers demanding 24/7 service. Business leaders pulled human resources to the table to make their companies better than the ones they read about and to provide overnight organizational capabilities. Finally, human resources was at the decision-making table and was a direct report of the CEO. The charge from the business leadership was to make sure that the workforce worked together more creatively, effectively and productively than the competition. Human resources was also expected to ensure total rewards aligned with business strategy, were implemented cost effectively and communicated to employees. HR would also develop appropriate performance management and succession planning while making the organization an employer of choice for whom everyone wanted to work. In the meantime, the government-mandated policing duties of the old personnel administration department were seamlessly integrated.

To make sure the seat at the table was not given to someone else, human resources leadership accepted the challenge in haste rather than risk being replaced. New titles emerged as "personnel" was replaced by "vice president of people"; "chief people officer"; "vice president, human capital"; "talent acquisition leader"; "talent development consultant"; and "vice president, talent." The same people who were in administrative and policing functions a decade before now had incredible goals to match their lofty new titles in their hard-won seats at the corporate table. Many of the business leaders expecting this transformation of their human resource departments worked in organizations that did not have the human resource information system infrastructure or the internal talent to expect the feats they read about in the business media. While the human resource staff struggled to integrate new strategic demands with routine administrative and regulatory tasks, budgets were cut, HR staff was reduced, and merger and acquisition activity increased. Not wanting to give up the coveted seat at the corporate table, human resources took on a fast-forward mentality and a reluctance to manage the expectations of senior management.

What Do You Want From HR Today?

The competitive business nature of the 1990s brought top human resources leaders into the direct reporting structure of the CEOs of most organizations. Previously, human resources reported to functions as varied as the COO, the legal department, vice president of administration or finance. After a history of monitoring compliance, human resource leaders landed in the boardroom as peers to those they once reported to, and in some companies, the reception was chilly at best. In the information- and knowledge-based economy of the '90s, the focus was on developing a customer-oriented workforce.

Mergers and acquisitions peaked during that decade, and human resource professionals without consulting budgets quickly became experts on the workforce implications of divestitures, mergers and acquisitions.

Recruiting, or talent acquisition, became a critical competency for human resources as "hot skills" in information technology and project management made these specialists scarce. Human resource professionals found themselves designing compensation packages to lure talent away from rivals while retaining their own top professionals. Job hunters increasingly began using the Internet to search for positions, and human resources' charge was to develop online recruiting strategies and an infrastructure to support them quickly and cost effectively. As the economy soared during the technology gold rush, human resources professionals and senior management read accounts of the recruiting prowess of high-tech companies like Microsoft, GE and PeopleSoft. The question to human resource professionals was, "Why can't we be more like them?"

One solution to the dilemma of managing administration and providing strategic human resource support was to outsource what business leaders considered "administrivia." The theory was that with an outside company handling employee benefits, payroll, relocation, HRIS, COBRA, flexible spending accounts, tuition reimbursement, transportation reimbursements, annual open enrollment and recruiting, companies would significantly decrease costs and gain expertise and technology not available in the current HR environment. Some companies expected to decrease head count in their human resource departments dramatically, and the remaining small, elite force would design and implement high-level, strategically-valued HR services. In reality, outsourcing did not necessarily live up to the theory. Human resources outsource providers found themselves in merger-and-acquisition mode throughout the '90s, while they redefined their service offerings and strategies. Managing service providers became yet another skill set that human resources had to quickly acquire while addressing change-management issues, both with their workforce and within the human resource department. Cost and customization became major issues in the early days of HR outsourcing.

As the e-business model moved into the rest of the organization, human resources functions that were not outsourced were expected to be online in an e-HR format. Information technology departments were charged with helping human resources transform into a paperless function with records, processes and online reporting. Issues of confidentiality, access and data security slowed down this effort in many organizations prior to privacy concerns. Between e-HR and outsourcing, surely human resources could meet a 1-to-200 ratio of HR staff-to-workforce and focus on strategic issues while saving companies hundreds of thousands of dollars in labor, space and technology. In many cases, this noble experiment failed, and organizations limped along with fractured versions of outsourcing, e-HR or a combination of these strategies.

Nearly half of senior executives are either dissatisfied with or ambivalent about the performance of their human resources departments, according to an independent survey of 150 U.S. senior executives released in July 2003 by Accenture, a human resource consulting and outsourcing concern. In the Accenture survey, forty-seven percent of senior executives said they were dissatisfied with or felt neutrally about the overall performance of their HR departments, while fifty-three percent said they were satisfied or extremely satisfied. The reason executives stated most often for their dissatisfaction was "response time," while "personal attention" and "access to information" were given as reasons for satisfaction with their HR departments.

According to a study released in August 2003 by Mercer Human Resources Consulting, one of the world's leading consulting organizations, the human resource function in most large U.S. organizations is in a state of significant transformation. Intense cost pressures drive this along with the growing recognition that an organization's workforce represents a new—and largely untapped—source of competitive advantage. Mercer surveyed HR leaders at more than 300 US-based organizations for six months to assess specific ways in which the HR function was changing, why the changes were occurring and what that meant for the broader organization. They released a report entitled "Transforming HR for Business Results: A Study of U.S. Organizations" to explain their findings. According to the study's author, David Knapp, a senior consultant in Mercer's technology and operations practice, "Maximizing the return on human capital investments has become a critical management and shareholder issue." Knapp expected companies' scrutiny of people-management practices and expectations of the HR function to play a more strategic role in achieving business success.

Human Resources' Smoldering Secret

If the profession is at a crossroads and has been for several years, the grim business realities of the early twenty-first century certainly have not made the role any easier for human resource professionals. After the September 11, 2001 terrorist attacks, a sluggish economy reversed the trends of the '90s. Human resource professionals were called on to design massive reductions in force. Workers were being called up for military duty. Some companies crashed in failure as corporate ethics violations were exposed by whistle blowers. As human resources departments faced staff reductions and budgets tightened even further, the role of people in organizations became more important than ever. HR was coping with the "survivor syndrome" of employees who escaped massive layoffs while also dealing with the loss of colleagues in their own department. During the transformation into strategic partner, human resources became the trauma team for workers frazzled by a technology meltdown, terrorism alerts and a stalled economy.

In the September 2003 "TP Track Survey" by Towers Perrin—one of the world's largest global management consulting firms, assisting organizations in managing people, performance and risk—human resources professionals were reportedly "struggling to do more with less." The report, titled "Tougher Times, Tougher HR," highlighted the responses of 265 North American human resources decision makers. The survey said that the respondents felt they were doing the best they could, considering the emerging gaps in needed competencies and constraints on spending. Respondents agreed that their staffs were feeling pressured and under stress, a finding consistent with the increased demands placed on the function today. Fifty-four percent reported their staff faced greater job stress today than they did eighteen months earlier, and fifty-seven percent agreed the day-to-day workload of their staff had increased. However, respondents saw improvements for their staffs in two areas: level of job challenge and increased interaction with senior management. In contrast with the Accenture survey, which indicated that senior executives were less than satisfied with the performance of the human resource function, "Tougher Times, Tougher HR" painted an interesting picture of the HR function. While feeling overworked, human resources professionals believed that they were effective in helping their organizations "weather these difficult times," said David Rhodes, a Towers Perrin principal who specializes in HR strategy and management.

Even though the sample sizes in all of the surveys were small, the reports consistently pointed to increased levels of stress for HR professionals. Along with budget constraints, reduced head count and line managers depending more and more on human resources to assist with people issues, the salary levels in the profession were stagnating. The 2002 "Human Resource Management Compensation Survey," which is considered the leading source of pay information for the HR profession, included data provided by nearly 1,100 U.S. employers that collectively have more than 10.3 million employees. The survey covered nearly 46,000 HR professionals in 109 HR jobs, ranging from top management to clerical positions. Among twelve of the most common jobs in HR, pay nudged up slightly for eleven of the twelve, for an average increase of 1.7 percent. The largest changes were for senior compensation analyst and general recruiter, both of which saw a 4.2 percent pay increase over 2001 pay levels. In the survey, the president of the Society of Human Resource Management (SHRM) commented that in recent years, compensation for HR professionals at all levels had been increasing steadily as a result of the increasing complexity and strategic nature of many HR roles. She expected to see improvements as the economy recovered.

The cover story of the July 2003 issue of *HRMagazine* was "Avoiding HR Burnout." While the workforce in general may be more fragile than it was a decade ago, human resources faces the pressure of transforming the profession with decreasing budgets and reduced staffs, in some cases lacking the skills for some of these new tasks. No large latitudinal studies have explored burnout among human resources employees, and letters to the editor following the *HRMagazine* article found many professionals dedicated to the field despite the challenges.

One human resource professional commented that while several strategic initiatives were being implemented within business units at her company, a new human resource information system was being implemented. There was a small budget for training and assistance from consultants. Her comment was that implementing a new system required full-time attention but no one was there to do their "day jobs," providing HRIS support for the business initiatives that could not fail. The information technology department was driving the timeline to launch the new system, so HR worked evenings and nights to test, configure and implement the new system. "It was not ideal, and it was more than stressful, but no one seemed to care. It had to get done, we did it, and it was expected," said the HR professional, who requested anonymity. She left the company after the HRIS system went "live' and still feels her sacrifices were largely unnoticed and there was not the type of recognition a business unit team would have received.

HR for HR: When the Advocate Needs an Advocate

In addition to the role human resources fills for management, there is also the role of employee advocate. The human resources professional employs effective listening, counseling, coaching and resolution of issues on behalf of employees in situations when line managers are unable to fill this role. But what happens to a human resources professional when he or she needs an advocate to navigate the realities of today's business environment? Organizations struggle with HR for HR.

Some organizations take the martyr's approach and claim that human resources professionals need no advocate. HR makes the policies in conjunction with management, they know the policies, and the policies are expected to provide any needed protection. This approach is reminiscent of the human-resources-as-administrative-cop mentality. While employees have both human resources and line managers to intervene on their behalf, human resource professionals in tough situations have no advocate. HR professionals are left to the whims of the business leaders they assist for feedback on their performance. In many organizations that embrace this martyr's approach, the succession plan for human resources is nonexistent, HR turnover is high, and burnout is even higher.

Other organizations appoint the chief human resources officer as the advocate for his or her human resources staff. One might call this the "Obi Wan Kenobi approach." Like the Jedi master from the *Star Wars* films, the head of human resources goes unchallenged in the assessment and mentorship of staff members. This makes sense in pure management terms—just as it does for line managers throughout the business—although there are times when even the chief people officer has biases toward or style differences with staff members that may cloud their effectiveness in finding the appropriate role for a team member. Sometimes there is conflict between human resources leaders and their peers in senior management. When senior managers challenge the human resources team, the HR leader must walk a fine line as an advocate for her own staff while maintaining accountability to her senior management peers. Another pitfall of the Obi Wan Kenobi approach in providing advocacy to human resources is that the department generally does not view the HR leader as an objective ombudsman.

In a profession going through transformation, achieving a seat at the coveted senior management table, increasing recognition of workforce needs from business leaders and an economy that fosters decreased human resources budgets and staff sizes, HR professionals need advocacy more than ever. Someone has to speak up and ensure that senior management expectations are in line with the infrastructure capabilities, staff competencies and line management support of the human resource department. If not, the risk of HR burnout increases significantly, and the profession risks losing talented individuals.

Complex Problems, Complex Solutions

Leading human resources through tumultuous times calls for HR leaders who combine results orientation with employee advocacy for their own staff (as well as the organization) and have the respect within their peer group to manage expectations. It also helps if human resource leaders can identify the signs of employee burnout and assist their line managers in understanding them and the serious consequences for morale and productivity.

Some of the most frequently mentioned signs of burnout are outlined in Table 1.

Table 1

Loss of productivity	Depression
Feelings of negativity toward the workplace	Tardiness
Negative and emotional outbursts	Use of drugs and alcohol
Changes in attitude	Poor quality work
Changes in work habits	Absenteeism
Fatigue	

Psychologists define burnout as the inability to relieve physical and mental symptoms associated with unrelenting stress. A more specific work-related definition by the National Institute for Occupational Safety and Health (NIOSH, 1999) calls work stress the harmful physical and emotional responses that occur when the requirements of the job do not match the capabilities, resources or needs of the worker. The ultimate result of stress is burnout, which can consist of emotional and physical exhaustion, emotional withdrawal, depersonalization and aggressive tendencies. Others refer to it simply as emotional exhaustion. No matter which definition is used, human resource leaders in many organizations have to increase their awareness of when the changes and demands of the profession—occurring at the same time as budget cutbacks and staff reductions—are increasing the risk of HR burnout. In addition to awareness, HR leaders are also charged with creating action plans to prevent, decrease and respond to work-related stress in their departments, just as they would the larger organization. According to Richard Leider, co-author of *Whistle While You Work: Heeding Your Life's Calling*, "The art of leadership is keeping tension between too little and too much stress."

From a human resources perspective, leaders realize that stress tolerance is individualized, and yet some companies develop a "burnout culture."

Psychologists Robert M. Yerkes and John D. Dodson studied the effects on stress and performance. In 1908, their work resulted in what is referred to as the Yerkes-Dodson Law. They concluded that at appropriate levels, stress increases both efficiency and performance. However, this relationship does not continue indefinitely in this fashion. When too many situations demand adjustment, stress exceeds a threshold. This stress overload contributes to diminishing performance, efficiency and even health. From a human resources perspective, leaders realize that stress tolerance is individualized, and yet some companies develop a "burnout culture." If there is a high incidence of stress-related illness, stress-induced Employee Assistance Plan (EAP) utilization, short-term disability utilization and work-related accidents in the general employee population, the HR department will generally mirror the same symptoms.

Competence Builds Confidence

Simply recognizing and addressing the signs of HR burnout and providing avenues for HR employee relation advocacy are not enough. HR leaders have to make sure that they have the right people in the right jobs and have realistic development plans in place to meet the demands of business leaders. In *The First 90 Days*, by Michael Watkins, the author suggests six employee categories for leaders to consider when restructuring: (1) keep in place; (2) keep and develop; (3) move to another position; (4) observe for a while; (5) replace, a low priority; and (6) replace, a high priority—put a new person in place as soon as possible. Although the intention is focused on new leaders, there is no reason that an existing HR manager couldn't use a similar model to evaluate staff based on changing business needs and expectations. Several work-related stress models indicate that when a job's demands exceed a person's knowledge, skills or preparation, he is at risk for burnout. In other words, there's a gap between what a person knows and what he is required to do. This knowledge or skill gap causes even greater stress and emotional harm when the results of mistakes are potentially serious.

In times of reduced HR budgets, training and development is often one of the first items cut. HR professionals are often directed to find in-house or local programs to meet their development needs. Based on business needs, this may not be a realistic option. More HR training options are available through teleseminars, video conferencing and webcasts. In coming years, HR e-learning opportunities are sure to increase. Another issue is determining the appropriate training for a human resource professional leading a business in transition. In cases where the HR professional has spent many years with one company or has been too busy to network, this becomes problematic. The HR professional doesn't know what he doesn't know. This is referred to as unconscious incompetence. The stress of a knowledge or skill gap can be particularly hard to deal with, because employees are often unable to identify particular skills or training that they are lacking. It is a Catch-22, because the HR professional is unaware of how little he actually knows about a topic until she begins to learn about that topic in depth. If a new HR leader brings experience from outside the organization, he can help professionals identify skill gaps. If the organization has an ongoing relationship with a consulting partner, the firm may have resources to provide or suggest training for the current staff based on business initiatives being implemented and observed HR competencies. Investing in the professional training and development of HR professionals to meet the demands of business leaders also helps the overall view of the department. The HR leader has to insure training investments are not limited to one or two high-potential employees and knowledge is transferred from consultants to the department.

Stress-Management Training

One sure way to elicit groans from the HR staff is to provide mandatory stress-management training. Many HR professionals believe they manage stress well; they are too experienced to benefit from stress-management training or attending training signifies weakness. In the corporate setting, human resource professionals interact directly with employees dealing with change, coping with layoffs and feeling insecure about the future. In some ways, HR professionals, especially employee relation specialists, are performing stress-filled roles, like health care workers or other professionals who deal with trauma. Studies on burnout began with professionals in the medical field and expanded to others with high people impact. Burnout starts with stress. If the HR leader can make a compelling case to members of the HR staff reminding them the current business environment has no precedent, department members may increase acceptance of training. It is imperative stress management training is conducted by a firm focused on and experienced with workplace stress. The credibility of the trainers and their program materials will also determine the acceptance of the message.

The goal of stress-management training is to help HR staff members prioritize, manage interruptions, develop conflict-management techniques and cope with the daily stress that will not go away.

Learning to manage stress in a way that is more than cosmetic is another step in preventing HR burnout. The goal of stress-management training is to help HR staff members prioritize, manage interruptions, develop conflict-management techniques and cope with the daily stress that will not go away. The HR staff will probably identify with some of the day-to-day pressure points that lead to a stressful work environment. A partial list of stressors is outlined in Table 2.

Table 2
Traits of a Stressful Work Environment

Constant interruptions	Continuous change
Time pressure deadlines	Too many internal meetings
Poor internal communication	Lack of support/resources to complete tasks
Poor leadership	Information overload
Office politics	

HR leaders can help manage stress at a departmental level by ensuring direct reports are communicating effectively as well as providing feedback, recognition and support to the people they supervise. While the HR leader has to keep the big picture in perspective and trust direct reports, it is important to stay connected with the HR staff. This gives the HR leader direct, unfiltered feedback from the front line. Heavy travel, meetings and a broad base of stakeholders make it easy for HR leaders to rely on department meetings as a way to connect with HR staff that are not direct reports. This may work in a smaller department; however, in larger HR departments, the leader will not get the input and perspective available at a more intimate luncheon or breakfast. Ideas from these gatherings can help the HR leader identify continuous improvements in decreasing stress at a departmental level.

An astute HR leader will notice some of the outward signs of stress in staff members. Changes in mood and/or behavior, irritability, increased absenteeism, deteriorating relationships with colleagues and reduced performance are some of the signs HR leadership will notice as employee stress levels increase. If one HR staff member is on short-term leave or suffers from a work-related, stress-induced illness, HR leadership should look at this as the tip of the iceberg. Even though one staff member may be exhibiting work-related stress symptoms or burnout, the HR leader may find severe stress throughout the department. Forward-thinking leaders must make the time to develop and implement an action plan to help lessen unnecessary stress within their departments. Some level of stress is expected when people work together, but the stress to avoid is the type that lowers the morale and productivity of the department.

The HR leader is a role model for the entire organization when it comes to the leadership of people. If the HR department members are burning out, department turnover is high, and performance for HR-aligned business partners declines; the HR leader has to address systemic department issues leading to work-related stress and burnout. The macho attitude that everyone should "grin and bear it" is outdated and can have a devastating impact on the HR department, the organization and external customer relationships in many ways. If senior managers are going to trust HR to lead the people of the organization, the HR leaders have to lead their departments in coping with the emerging issue of work-related stress leading to burnout.

Harnessing e-HR without Wearing the Harness

Technology is supposedly the answer to all human resource woes, from work-related stress and HR burnout to transforming organizational culture. When the department can implement the latest HR technology, half the department will disappear, paper-based tasks will be completed online, and HR will have time on its hands to design and implement strategic initiatives to help the organization face external business challenges. It is a fantasy, of course, and before the organization commits to spending millions of dollars on hardware and software, HR owes senior management a glimpse of how it will work. Electronic human resources, or e-HR, means different things to different HR leaders. One definition is the application of technology—the Internet, corporate intranet or wireless technology—to administer, communicate and deliver human resource information or tools.

Many times, HR technology assumes a great deal of data entry responsibility will shift to the employee or line-management. In some organizations, this may work, while in others, it backfires. If there is paperwork or processes line managers currently completed in HR, when the work is transitioned to line management, there is resentment. Line managers often feel the human resources department is putting work on their desks. While HR sees a technology implementation as a great step forward, business leaders may see it as HR relieving its pressure by passing the buck. Similar issues occur when employee self-service is implemented within an organizational culture that does not invest in change management training before the process moves from HR to the workforce. Employee resentment results and the HR leader and staff have to sometimes "sell" the benefit of having processes close to owners of the data.

In other implementations, the technology is not everything it is supposed to be. What is sold as a streamlined, easy-to-use system is often an inflexible, table-driven software package with multiple, mandatory upgrades intended to suck dollars from the organization and work hours from IT and HRIS staff. Implementing "vanilla" software packages to avoid customization may require complex reworking of current processes. HR leaders generally leave technical detail to IT and HRIS staff while they focus on financial considerations. Nothing hurts an HR leader's credibility more than convincing senior management peers that an investment in HR technology will yield improvements that ultimately never materialize. The HR leader has to get a "real-world" idea of what the end product will look like in the hands of senior management, HR staff, line management and employees. The only way to do that is to add to an already heavy travel schedule a trip to a live site running the same software on the same platform (not a beta site or a corporate demo).

Technology can be cumbersome and is generally expensive, but it may answer multiple problems and provide the HR department some relief to focus on more strategic business issues.

Technology can be cumbersome and is generally expensive, but it may answer multiple problems and provide the HR department some relief to focus on more strategic business issues. In many organizations, experience and competence around e-HR does not exist. The IT and HR departments have read about it and heard about it, but they have been living with the current system. The HR leader may hire someone with expertise working in a more automated environment to join the team or may rely on an existing consulting relationship to assess the current situation and guide the organization to e-HR solutions. One goal is to ensure necessary planning, training and change management for the organization, and HR is part of the investment plan. HR staff, executives, line managers and employees have to understand the expectations of their interaction with the technology prior to implementation.

Human Resource Executive magazine and ERC/Dataplus surveyed 581 human resource professionals in 2001. Eighty-two percent of the respondents found that intranet technology had not significantly reduced their workload at that time. Watson Wyatt, a global consulting firm specializing in human capital and financial management, conducted an e-HR survey in 2002. Based on responses from 649 companies, it tracked how employers had invested in e-HR initiatives and how each organization had benefited from those investments. Their research identified three "best e-HR practices" consistently used by high-performing organizations that report better results on HR efficiencies and employee satisfaction levels. These practices include having a formal, documented e-HR strategy that is supported by senior management and key stakeholders; a sound business case for e-HR investments; and, a best-fit approach to selecting and integrating a mix of HR systems, applications and sourcing strategies. Technology is another area where the changes in the business environment are leading human resource departments to make rapid changes to meet the needs of the organization.

Outsourcing: HR to Go

Rather than cope with HR burnout, the cost of HR technology investments and building competence within the current organization, some senior managers have decided it is easier to outsource the human resource function. In 2000, Exult, a human resource business processing outsourcing supplier, went public, and it looked like the human resources profession would be changed forever. While professional employer organizations (PEOs) were providing cost savings in employee benefits and increasing market share with smaller companies, there was not a PEO equivalent for larger organizations. Exult answered that perceived need. They focused on large companies; its client roster includes BP, Bank of America, Prudential Financial, International Paper, BMO Financial Group, Universal Music Group and McKesson. In addition to finance and accounting processes like accounts payable, travel and expenses and general accounting, Exult provides human resources processes including:

- Payroll
- Benefits administration
- Recruiting and staffing
- Relocation and expatriate support
- Learning (training)
- Employee contact centers (call centers)

Chapter Four

Foundations For Diversity

Benjamin F. Brooks, BA

"Diversity" is perhaps one of the most loaded words in the English language. Pregnant with possibility, bathed in misperceptions and tarnished by ill use, the word can conjure up a tense tangle of emotions within the average American. Such emotionalism derails any logical attempt at a realistic and objective inclusion of diversity into the American workplace and social consciousness. Too often, we bring with us preconceived baggage—established boundaries and engendered prejudices—that cloud any attempt at understanding and practicing the art of diversity. We live and work in a very "politically correct" world, where businesspeople claim to promote diversity in the workplace. But do we really understand what diversity means?

What comes to mind when you think of diversity? Although the word is pluralistic in nature, we tend to define diversity in very limiting terms. We see diversity as an effort to tie together very dichotomous issues. The average American thinks of diversity and immediately conjures up categories such as "black-white" and "male-female." That's where the misperceptions and anxiety over diversity lie, inadvertently bringing an "us vs. them" mentality to the word. When the word diversity is mentioned in conversation, dialogue is usually centered upon this two-sided premise. People can also mistakenly see diversity as a dangerous threat to the established power structure—not as a viable method for inclusion, self-enhancement and corporate growth.

During my many years of involvement in diversity awareness education and training, I have come to a very interesting and perhaps startling conclusion. Diversity is not a black-white, male-female issue. It is a people issue—the one true thing we all have in common. Until we begin to approach it as a people issue, common to us all, confusion will reign. When I was asked to write this chapter, I jumped at the opportunity to address some of the basic, elementary facts necessary to develop a true concept of diversity. I hope this chapter will bring a more realistic perspective to the issue of diversity and promote its healthy practice. A heightened sense of diversity can empower employees and create a more productive workplace.

In order for us to appreciate diversity awareness education, we must know what diversity really means and how it impacts the business environment. One of the most concise definitions of diversity that I have seen comes from Thomas S. Watson, Jr., a diversity awareness author. In his book *Connecting People: Discovering Peace and Power Through Cultural Flexibility*, Watson describes cultural diversity as "an environment in which people of differing backgrounds teach, learn, live, work, worship, and otherwise communicate with each other" (Watson, p. 113). This simple definition describes diversity in its ideal state; when read aloud in a diversity awareness seminar, these words would not raise any eyebrows. We know, however, that we don't live an in ideal, unbiased world. Remember that when confronted with the concept of diversity, we often bring with us preconceived baggage that taints our view. Watson tells us that our real-world approach to diversity can be helped or hindered by the following components: cultural arrogance, sensitivity and flexibility (Watson 113).

Cultural arrogance can be defined as "the mental habit of allowing obsession with superficial differences of others to destroy communication" (Watson 113). Such arrogance can muddy any attempt to introduce diversity into a workplace environment. Cultural arrogance is not necessarily a conscious reaction to a situation. Due to ingrained social programming, it is often very difficult for us to understand or accept anyone or anything that does not fit comfortably within our frame of reference. Have you ever made preconceived assumptions about someone before you really had gotten a chance to know him or her, perhaps based on a foreign or regional accent? That's cultural arrogance in action, no matter how harmless it seems.

To a greater extreme, the "English Only" rule in the workplace reflects the drive toward the safety of ethnocentrism. What spurs such rules? Is it an economic or safety issue? Perhaps this rule is generated by the overarching fear of not being able to monitor conversations—the fear that "they" are talking about "us." As long as these attitudes exist based on superficial differences such as language, skin color or physical disabilities, cultural arrogance will become a permanent barrier to understanding issues of diversity.

Now that we know about the barrier of cultural arrogance, what roles do sensitivity and flexibility play in our efforts to create a diverse environment? Cultural sensitivity is "the ability to understand and empathize with a person or group of people whose demonstrated values, way of life, religion, conventions and possibly language are different from your own" (Watson 113). Until we are truly ready to see the world through someone else's eyes, it is very difficult to fully understand and appreciate this aspect of diversity. Many diversity practitioners emphasize treating people the way you would like to be treated. Tony Alessandra, a member of the National Speaker's Association, shifts the parameters slightly by reminding us to "treat people the way *they* would like to be treated." The only way this can be accomplished is through educating yourself about the individual or the individual's cultural background. The cherished maxim about "walking a mile in someone else's shoes" has never before been so true.

"A mind that is stretched by an idea will
never assume its original shape."

—*The late Justice Oliver Wendell Holmes*

Cultural flexibility is "the mental habit of overlooking superficial differences of physical appearance, personal beliefs, dietary preferences and lifestyles to find a basis for mutual respect and communication" (Watson, p. 113). To be successful in an increasingly multicultural America, organizations must be able to adjust or adapt to new workplace situations, employee differences and even diversity within their client base. The late Justice Oliver Wendell Holmes said, "A mind that is stretched by an idea will never assume its original shape." Flexibility will become the oil that lubricates the future organization's machinery. As we move further into the 21st century, managers and supervisors across all industries who are able to speak, write and perform in a culturally flexible manner will be very much in demand. Those who do not fully and objectively embrace the philosophy of diversity will be as useless as a sundial in the shade.

In *Fatal Illusions: Shredding a Dozen Unrealities That Can Keep Your Organization From Success*, James R. Lucas tells us that "victory generally comes from successfully exploiting contrasts rather than from ensuring performance similarities" (Lucas 111). Too many companies try to fit their employees—and even their client base—into a preconceived mold, thus creating a false sense of corporate unity. We tend to create false beliefs regarding what our organizations are like and the direction in which they are going. To increase our comfort level, we fall prey to the erroneous assumption that we know what other people are thinking rather than acknowledging what we do not know and benefiting from our differences. As a business professional, the big question you must ask yourself is, "How can I best serve my customers if I don't understand what makes them tick?"

Now that we have a working definition of diversity, how do we create a comprehensive, educational awareness base that encourages organizational effectiveness? Just as a builder lays out his blueprints for constructing a building, we must start with a solid foundation for diversity education. If the proper building blocks are not used, our builder's structure will crumble when the first storm hits rather than stand the test of time. As a diversity practitioner, I will share with you the basic building blocks for any successful diversity awareness education program. If implemented properly, the following building blocks can give you the strength to ride out any storm:

- Attitude
- Self-Esteem
- Communication
- Customer Service/Satisfaction
- Teamwork/Partnership
- Vision
- Problem Solving
- Commitment

ATTITUDE

Everything we do in life begins and ends with attitude. I always start my training sessions with these words: "So what's the importance of attitude?" Ask any Fortune 500 executive or professional athlete and they'll tell you that they couldn't have gotten where they are now without it. Attitude shapes not only how we see ourselves and the world around us but how the world perceives us. Many people simply cannot comprehend the vast impact that their attitude has on every human contact. In an effort to capture the influence of attitude in tangible terms, researchers at the Carnegie Institute of Technology embarked on a landmark study that yielded truly remarkable results. They found that fifteen percent of the success that one enjoys in life is directly related to one's technical skills and mental ability. Eighty-five percent of the success is directly related to how well that person deals with other people (Giblin 4).

Many people simply cannot comprehend the vast impact that their attitude has on every human contact.

Motivational speaker Zig Ziglar is fond of declaring, "It's your attitude, not just your aptitude that determines your ultimate altitude." No matter how smart you think you may be, without a positive attitude, you will be tethered to the ground. In today's demanding and diverse business environment, developing a positive attitude is a critical element for success, not only for yourself but also for your employees.

During one of my recent training sessions, a young woman in the audience raised her hand as I talked about the importance of a positive attitude. She wanted to know how she could maintain a positive attitude while fellow co-workers exhibited a "gloom and doom" demeanor on a daily basis. As she spoke, I could readily identify with what she was saying. Immediately upon entering the building to go to the classroom, I had observed many of the people to whom she was referring.

I often like to share the following metaphor with anyone who wants to develop and maintain a positive attitude. Picture yourself entering a very dark room where you know that other people are waiting patiently, but you are unable to see anyone. Upon entering the room, you are given a lighted candle. At that point, your small but steady light allows everyone to see faintly. Someone quickly approaches and attempts to blow out your candle. No matter how and when you attempt to re-light your candle, someone else is there, ready to blow it out again. You immediately seek out ways to shield your candle. Imagine the parallel in your own life. As we move through life, we encounter negative individuals basking in their own inner darkness, who want to blow out our proverbial candles. This may happen when you get a position that someone else wanted. Maybe you have a special talent that makes another person jealous. Myriad things within the workplace can trigger such ugly reactions from co-workers. Such repetitive behaviors can plunge a whole organization into darkness over the course of time.

Having a clear understanding of yourself and the implications of your own attitude can give you the strength to prevent anyone from impacting your lighted candle. Part of this process involves developing positive daily affirmations. When the antagonists in your life discover that they cannot blow out your candle, no matter how hard they try, their behavior will cease. At the same time, they may begin to realize the efforts you made to keep your candle lit. People tend to imitate success. You will soon discover that your ability to keep your candle lit will encourage someone else in the crowd to light his or her own candle. Before long, others will follow suit. In a short time, the dark room you first entered will be completely illuminated. Just think—it all started with one person lighting a solitary candle!

Every person has a candle deep within. For numerous reasons, such as fear of failure or negative self-worth, people are often afraid to light their candles. Perhaps they've had their candles blown out by past supervisors who told them that they didn't have the experience or education needed to accomplish a certain job goal. Or maybe they didn't feel like they fit in among other staff members for reasons of color, ethnicity or disability. Employees are waiting to see if we as supervisors and managers light our own candles. If we can maintain a positive attitude and openly share it with others, we have the ability to inspire our employees to display their own light.

In order to develop and maintain a positive attitude, one must understand the complexity of our working relationships along with the personal issues that the modern worker brings with him or her to the office, store or factory every day. How we respond to these issues will make a huge difference in employee attitude. When supervisors and managers recognize the necessity of helping their staffs deal with challenges in their personal lives as well as in their professional lives, they begin to understand the full impact they have in shaping attitudes. It is very difficult for management to influence the attitudes of others when they are not fully aware of how to effectively deal with people issues. Managers must be empathetic and have the ability to view situations from the other side of the table.

Management can shape employee attitudes through the positive introduction of diversity awareness education. When diversity is looked upon as something that has been thrust upon employees, the reaction is manifested in the form of negative attitudes. When people feel valued, it is reflected in their attitudes and workplace behavior. When they believe they are devalued, the opposite is true. Therefore, the best way to introduce diversity awareness education into the workplace is based on understanding how people behave when they feel both valued and devalued. Managers and supervisors need to develop a clear understanding of people issues and how these issues impact the creation of a diverse environment.

Not only will developing and maintaining a positive attitude assure increased personal success, but your actions will rub off on employees and clients. I've create five steps that can easily be incorporated into your daily life:

- Great each person you meet as if he (or she) were a long-lost friend.
- Give him a firm handshake and a welcoming smile.
- Find something good about the individual and compliment them.
- Display a positive attitude throughout the day, even when things get tough.
- Treat everyone with dignity, respect and self-worth.

There's an old adage that says attitudes are contagious. Is yours worth catching?

SELF-ESTEEM

At this point, you may be asking yourself, "So why are there so many people in the world with bad attitudes? And why do they keep trying to blow out my candle?" Negative attitudes typically start with low self-esteem. Self-esteem is how one feels about oneself deep down inside. Negative or positive self-views shape the attitude we outwardly display to others. If you feel poorly about yourself, how can you possibly feel good about other people? Poor self-esteem spreads as rapidly as negative attitudes. If you encounter a manager or supervisor who does not feel good about himself, chances are high that his direct subordinates will reflect their boss's negative feelings in their own work and attitude toward others.

The higher the level of self-esteem, the more likely one will be to treat others with tolerance, respect, kindness and generosity. Individuals with high self-esteem tend to have greater levels of self-motivation and are more willing to accept responsibility for their actions and take pride in their accomplishments. Individuals with high self-esteem are also good at handling constructive criticism.

Educational consultants and researchers Drs. James Levin and John Shanken-Kaye created a compelling formula that deconstructs the elements that contribute to self-esteem (Levin and Shanken-Kaye 33). The formula is:

Self-Esteem = Significance + Competence + Virtue + Power

Boosting the self-esteem of your workforce is not only essential to greater productivity but to the successful implementation of diversity awareness education. For this reason, let's break down the formula developed by Levin and Shanken-Kaye and view it within the concept of diversity.

Significance

Significance represents an individual's sense of personal importance and acceptance within a larger community. When a minority individual enters the workplace, there is an immediate search not just for a friendly face but a similar face. Even as an experienced diversity practitioner, I still find myself searching for a familiar face of color when I enter a new environment. Why? Quite simply, there is a certain comfort level in knowing that you are not alone. We look for the familiar and the trusted when thrown into unaccustomed situations or new environments, and we search for an instant sense of belonging. This phenomenon can be seen in workplaces across the United States as employees of the same ethnic backgrounds congregate together during the lunch hour.

We look for the familiar and the trusted when thrown into unaccustomed situations or new environments, and we search for an instant sense of belonging.

I'm reminded of the book entitled *Why Are All the Black Kids Sitting Together in the Cafeteria?* and *Other Conversations About Race: A Psychologist Explains the Development of Racial Identity* by Beverly Daniel Tatum. In countless school cafeterias and office lunchrooms throughout the United States, individuals who have difficulty with the concept of inclusion quietly whisper this question. Such people normally reason that this practice represents another fine example of people who claim to want an integrated society yet eagerly find ways of systematically separating themselves. People who make this rather shortsighted argument fail to notice that beyond the small group of African American workers, there are tables of whites sitting by themselves. Ironically, these individuals see nothing unusual or limiting about that behavior. How do we break this chain that separates us? There is a term in social psychology called "propinquity increases attraction." This means that the more we interact with each other—no matter how different we appear—we can create a stronger bond. The simple solution for those critical of the workers sitting alone is to ask to join them.

Breaking out of our comfort zones in order to experience new people and situations can be a nerve-wracking task, due largely to a lifetime of exposure to conscious and unconscious cultural programming. An experience that happened to me long ago in childhood still stays with me as a vivid example of how cultural programming and loss of community can effect one's sense of significance. As a child growing up in North Carolina, I worked in the tobacco fields with family and friends during the summer months. One of our neighbors was responsible for getting together all the field hands needed to work for various farmers. One hot summer day, I was the only one from our community to show up for work. When the truck arrived, I was taken to the work site. When I arrived, I blinked in fearful disbelief. I scanned the group for a familiar-looking face; only white faces peered back. That day, I was the only African-American working at this location. An immediate feeling of depression swept over me during our ride to the tobacco fields. It was the first time in my life that I found myself in an all-white environment. I was paralyzed with fear and dread. I didn't eat a bit of food all day, because my stomach was tied up in tense, painful knots. An agonizing and endless day of mental anguish unfolded before me.

> Too often, the barriers we put up in an attempt to protect
> ourselves can limit us just as much as those
> constructed by others.

Based on the strength of my response, you may assume I experienced racial slurs or threats of physical violence by the other workers. I have to answer in the negative. Absolutely no racial comments were made against me. There was also nothing to indicate any difficulty between my fellow workers and myself. I didn't look like them, but on that day, nobody seemed to care, with the exception of one person—me.

I swore a silent oath as I firmly promised myself, "If I ever get over this day, I will never allow myself to be in a situation like this again!" Little did I realize that that experience would set the course for a lifetime of operating in a diverse environment. Too often, the barriers we put up in an attempt to protect ourselves can limit us just as much as those constructed by others.

As a manager in a diverse workplace, it is your responsibility to help your personnel expand their sense of significance. In fact, truly great leaders go out of their way to boost the self-esteem of their staff. If people believe in themselves and feel accepted as crucial members of the work team, it's amazing what they can accomplish. Self-esteem building begins when you meet a new employee, especially if that individual is a minority worker. Meeting one's manager or supervisor for the first time can either be a traumatic or rewarding experience, setting the tone for ongoing workplace relations. When a minority worker has a feeling of acceptance, that person's productivity will rise. In turn, this increases your organization's competitive advantage. If a supervisor or manager behaves in an alienating manner, you can expect permanent damage to the propagation of a multicultural work environment as well as employee productivity.

Competence

Somewhere along the line, competence has erroneously become a dirty word. When someone is not working to the best of their ability, They are deemed merely "competent." What does the word "competence" mean to you, and what do you expect from your employees? Do you view it as going above and beyond job responsibilities or merely getting by until the clock strikes five? Most importantly, what do you expect of yourself as a manager?

If you work in a management capacity, your most important function lies in the development of your people. Management must encourage high levels of competence in individuals for the betterment of the organization. When employees view themselves as competent, there is a rise in their self-esteem. Encouraging high levels of competence also means having to hold subordinates directly accountable for bad work or poor decisions, regardless of race, ethnicity or gender. However, managers and supervisors within a multicultural workplace are often hesitant to take such actions. When a person of color is employed, often there is a culturally programmed reluctance on the part of the white supervisor to hold the minority worker's feet to the fire for fear of appearing biased. External features like skin pigmentation do not attest to the competence or organizational effectiveness of any particular person or group. The same scenario can be applied to an employee who has a physical disability or to a female employee working in an all-male environment. Consequently, the standard of performance expected from an employee should be based on the job description and established performance factors—not on how that employee looks. Acting otherwise is a disservice to both the organization and its employees.

If you work in a management capacity, your most important function lies in the development of your people.

Virtue

Levin and Shankin-Kaye define virtue as "a person's perceived feeling of worthiness as a result of their ability and willingness to help others" (Levin and Shankin-Kaye 33). Viewing this definition within the framework of diversity awareness education, I have found that the concepts of virtue and value are inexorably linked. A person's value is based upon the uniqueness of their skill, the demand for their service and the difficulty in replacing them (Nightingale). A model workplace is one in which a manager shows both the ability and willingness to help people on the path to success. By showing such willingness, you can encourage others to find their own unique sense of value and virtue within the larger organization.

As a manager or supervisor, do you have a certain skill that makes you unique or irreplaceable? Perhaps it's your ability to handle people. Ironically, too many managers lack the ability to effectively relate to their workforce, something that I deem the most vital prerequisite to successful leadership. Even further, the truly successful leader has the ability to target and bring out the value in his or her personnel.

When you find a way to connect with your workers, you become indispensable.

The ability to build a sense of individual value within yourself and your workforce is of critical importance, especially in today's era of corporate downsizing. When I hear someone worry over a possible job loss, I remind that person of his or her value and marketability. We define our jobs; our jobs mustn't define us. To become viable members of the 21st century workforce, we must be willing to continually reinvent ourselves to respond to the changing needs around us. For example, individuals in management positions who have demonstrated cultural flexibility and the ability to handle people within diverse environments are difficult to replace. Managers who are multilingual gain an added advantage. In today's rapidly shrinking and increasingly interconnected world, international social, political and economic forces have a powerful impact on our daily lives.

When you find a way to connect with your workers,
you become indispensable.

Is the typical American worker ready to engage the world? The rest of the world has long understood the essential value in learning as many languages as possible. However, our geographic distance from other countries, combined with the longtime prevalence of English as the dominant language in international business dealings, has given Americans a sense of complacency with regard to learning new languages. Organizations that wish to remain competitive in an increasingly global environment will aggressively seek out individuals with the skills necessary to interact with diverse clients and business partners.

Power

Undeniably, the locus of power lies at the top of every organization. However, it is important for every employee to learn how to cultivate a positive sense of power and control within his/her workplace environment. Levin and Shanken-Kaye define power as "a person's perception that she exerts control over important aspects of her environment" (Levin and Shanken-Kaye 33). Managers must continually strive to show employees at every level how to develop personal as well as organizational power to create a truly passionate and productive corporate community. When individuals develop a true sense of power, they gain a stronger sense of responsibility, which can and will be reflected in the quality of their work.

Creating an empowering environment for improved employee performance involves building up people's sense of self-esteem and value. Instead of just delegating projects or responsibilities without any dialogue, why not ask employees what actions they feel are necessary to make a project run smoothly? You may be surprised by their answers; they might supply new solutions to old problems. Once you involve people in the process, find examples of what your employees are doing right and share these observations with them. This involves reinforcing the positive aspects of people's skills and abilities and reminding them of the critical ways in which these abilities contribute to the greater good of the organization. When people have a sense of power over a situation, they are more likely to be committed to improving the final outcome.

Creating an empowering environment for improved
employee performance involves building up people's
sense of self-esteem and value.

Are you doing enough to build your group's sense of power? You can start by incorporating these elements into your management style:

- Touch people in a way that makes them feel like vital parts of the organization.
- Continually reinforce positive aspects of their abilities.
- Openly demonstrate confidence in your own abilities; employees will take notice.
- Encourage positive daily affirmations.

You are the example. Never forget that you set the benchmark for quality and success.

COMMUNICATION

A social revolution is occurring across the United States as organizations are forced to communicate much differently today than in the past. A nationwide survey showed that executives believe that fourteen percent of each forty-hour workweek is wasted due to poor communication between staff and managers, amounting to an astounding seven weeks per year. The survey, developed by OfficeTeam of Menlo Park, California, asked 150 executives from large companies to estimate how much time was wasted. The mean response was fourteen percent ("Are you wasting seven weeks a year?"). The traditional and highly bureaucratic top-down communications model is steadily being abandoned for an open, two-way communication style. The fluidity of information in business today, combined with an increasingly educated and diverse workforce, is convincing leaders that effective organizational communication goes two ways.

Management can reap maximum effectiveness from personnel by developing open channels of communication throughout the organizational network. In the two-way communication model, managers must become masterful listeners; they need to be able to receive as well as send. Effective internal communications start with incorporating basic skills such as listening, speaking, questioning and sharing feedback within the daily work environment. By listening and responding, the manager is able to harness the interests and energies of employees, which can result in increasing focus, productivity and innovation. When a strong communications system is in place, employees have a clearer understanding of their roles and responsibilities. Employees also gain a better understanding of the vision and mission of the organization. If a good mission statement is in place, the employee will strive toward higher levels of customer satisfaction.

Managers and supervisors also must learn how to communicate across cultural lines, without letting cultural arrogance creep into the communications process.

With today's increasingly diverse workforce, it's easy to believe that you have conveyed information to someone when, in fact, that person may have interpreted your message differently than you intended. Unfortunately, you won't be aware of this problem until a major problem or issue arises out of the confusion. Managers and supervisors also must learn how to communicate across cultural lines, without letting cultural arrogance creep into the communications process. I once taught a diversity training class consisting of a group of highway workers. These workers clearly did not appreciate or welcome the concept of diversity within their workplace. They bemoaned the fact that there were several individuals on the highway team who lacked a mastery of the English language. "Anyone who comes to this country should be able to speak the language," they argued. Another worker added, "Why should we have to worry about helping them? We've got our own jobs to do!" People who take the same attitude as these highway workers believe that everyone must adjust to them; they see no point in making their own adjustments. Cultural flexibility demands that accommodations must be made for success. What I found most disturbing about this encounter was that their manager (who was also present) shared the same viewpoint. Employees will mirror the attitudes of management.

Strong communication networks are essential to every organization. However, organizations with a diverse work force must take an added step by ensuring that a clear, effective, cross-cultural communications system is in place. Dr. Alan Weiss, author of Rejoicing in Diversity, states, "Sensitivity to people who are different from you—in whatever manner—is not an endemic human trait. You must discipline yourself to exhibit sensitivity, no less than you discipline yourself to be service-oriented with customers or to return phone calls promptly" (Weiss).

A key ingredient to developing effective communications, especially in a diverse work environment, is to make it a part of everyday activities. Management must stay involved with every level of personnel, including front-line staff. When assigning a task to your subordinates, ask them to paraphrase the duty you instructed them to perform and inquire if there are any questions. If you make this a constant procedure for all employees, you give everyone a chance to state if something is unclear without fear or embarrassment. It's also a helpful practice for supervisors to meet with their employees at least once a month to make sure that workplace activities are on track and to hear any current concerns. Listen closely to suggestions on how you could communicate more effectively. This cultivates a firm sense of cultural flexibility and creates an important bond between supervisor and employee.

Here are some key points to remember:

- Understanding is the first step in good communicating.
- After you understand, seek to be understood.
- Always strive for a win-win outcome.
- Remember that there is always a possibility of misunderstanding in any communication; be tolerant and flexible.
- Ask the person to paraphrase what you said to ensure that he or she really understands.

CUSTOMER SERVICE/SATISFACTION

Customer service is a term that every organization proudly espouses as vital to operations; however, very few really perceive its true significance or its limitations. Throughout Corporate America, the term "customer service" gets wrapped up in sleek marketing campaigns and slipped into the polished mission and vision statements without a thought to its meaning. Even further, only a sparse number of organizations can claim to understand the difference between customer service and customer satisfaction. Customer service is seen as having employees available to answer a few questions or directing customers to the right product. An indifferent belief exists within many organizations that little needs to be done to keep a customer; if a good product is offered, the customer will return, regardless of the level of customer service. Customer service gets the customer; customer satisfaction keeps him.

Customer service gets the customer;
customer satisfaction keeps him.

Organizations fail to understand the full impact that employee actions have on their bottom line, particularly in a multicultural environment. When reviewing your customer service/satisfaction program, consider these points:

- Always remember that your position would not exist if it were not for the customer. Realize the important role that the customer plays in your multicultural employment.

- Your employees speak for your company louder than you will ever know.

- The internal customer is equally as important as the external customer. The treatment of your personnel has a direct impact on how they interact with your external customers.

- When you walk out of your company's doors (for lunch or at the end of the day), you become the customer. How did the person behind the counter at your local deli, gas station or dry cleaner treat you today? What did you like or dislike about his/her behavior? Compare this to how you treat your customers.

- Your organization's success will be realized when customer service is coupled with customer satisfaction.

TEAMWORK/PARTNERSHIPS

In the wild, the cheetah is reputed to be one of the fastest animals alive. It can attain speeds of up to sixty miles per hour in agile pursuit of its prey. However, in spite of its exceptional speed, it only makes a kill one time out of four, which means that at some point, the animal will go hungry. Now look at the hyena and the other wild dogs that hunt in the same environment as the cheetah. Studies show they can be assured a 100 percent kill rate. They do not have the cheetah's immense speed and agility on their side, but what they do have is teamwork. Evolution and experience have taught these animals that if each member of the pack does its individual part, the task will be accomplished.

In the world of business (and sports), teamwork is also necessary for survival. But great teams don't happen without concerted effort. They result from hard work and a purposeful, deliberate effort on the part of leaders and team members to come together around a common vision. One of the best examples of effective teamwork I've seen involves the efforts of the Chicago Bulls basketball team under the stewardship of coach Phil Jackson. He brought together different personalities in order to create a championship-winning team.

As a team leader and coach, success begins with realizing that you "need to include team members who may not have the right credentials but who have great interest in the effort. They can bring not only necessary fire to their role but also a fresh perspective, because they haven't been locked into what is 'doable'" (Lucas 126). The manager or supervisor who realizes this will be the one who places his company in the best competitive position. There are too many managers and supervisors who marginalize employees on a daily basis, totally ignoring the contributions they can make to the organization's goals and objectives. This behavior not only stunts the individual's potential but also severely handicaps the team.

As a team leader and coach, success begins with realizing that you "need to include team members who may not have the right credentials but who have great interest in the effort."

In our diverse work environments, it is critical for an organization to carefully examine the mix of its work teams. "Matching rather than 'assigning' people to projects and teams is crucial for success," James Lucas reminds us (Lucas 126). Recognizing how each culture can bring its own perspective to the work team, one must know how to build an environment in which each perspective is honored and valued. Management also must instill in workers the critical role each person plays in his/her team. If team members feel they are stakeholders in developing and articulating the company's goals and vision, they will more likely express project commitment and motivation. Creating a diverse team responsive to individual needs and organizational growth requires dialogue, a willingness to listen nonjudgmentally to ideas and a skillful leader to help guide the team toward its goals. This leader must find ways to best utilize the unique talents and personalities of team members. One must incorporate all perspectives to get good results. The next time you are called upon to draft key players, keep this in mind:

When you pick the team that you like,
you become popular.
When you pick a team that you need,
you become successful.

As your team's coach, make these points part of your game plan:

- There is no "I" in TEAM.
- Every member plays a key and significant role.
- Synergy on the team is critically important.
- Team cohesion is essential.
- You win or lose as a team.

VISION

Too often, organizations draft lofty vision statements that are sorely disconnected from the realities of the workplace. Such vision statements, constructed by senior-level executives, never really find their way down to the front-line worker. They generally contain generic goals (such as becoming an industry leader) but lack a clear action plan that incorporates issues affecting their workforce or client base. In most cases, there is little opportunity for employees to ask questions about the vision or challenge the vision, particularly at the lower levels in the organization. In turn, most personnel feel that they are not real stakeholders in the corporate vision. If employees are unable to take personal ownership of their company's vision, it is unlikely that they will want to embody the company's vision in the daily work environment. Companies that lack a clear sense of vision are traveling down a dangerous path. In this era of economic uncertainty, we've witnessed several prominent examples of companies that failed because they were unable to keep an eye on their competition and update their vision to fit changing socioeconomic realities. When a company cannot articulate its vision, especially to its employees, it can become blind-sided by the competition.

Corporate vision should be viewed as an ongoing and
dynamic process rather than words cast in stone.

Vision statements are meant to expand our thinking and break us free from preconceived boundaries by providing us with a true sense of direction and purpose. In Fatal Illusions, James Lucas reminds us that a vision statement should guide us to where we want to go, either as individuals or as organizations (Lucas 45). Like following a road map, we are lost if we are not furnished with enough details. Companies that wish to offer a true sense of inclusion and diversity awareness should build vision statements that can truly be shared and embraced by all employees. Finally, corporate vision should be viewed as an ongoing and dynamic process rather than words cast in stone. Companies must be willing to revise their vision statements based on internal and external challenges in order to stay ahead of the competition.

When evaluating the strength of your organization's vision, keep the following points in mind:

- If there is no vision, you operate like a rudderless ship.
- Employees need to see where the organization is going.
- Your vision allows you to fix your sight on the ultimate goal.
- If you can't visualize the goal, how can you communicate it to your people?
- Without a clear vision, your organization is headed for economic disaster.

PROBLEM SOLVING

Have you ever heard the old joke, "How do you eat an elephant?" The answer, of course, is "one bite at a time." Creating a course of effective problem solving, especially within a diverse workplace, is akin to eating an elephant one bite at a time. Don't expect to solve a workplace dilemma in one sitting. As a manager, you will face problems that seem to pop out of nowhere. However, upon further exploration, you will find that many of your most daunting workplace problems have been allowed to gestate over time. Such problems may have been ignored or underestimated by the organization until it suddenly becomes clear that you have what amounts to a 3,000-pound elephant sitting on your desk, demanding your immediate attention.

Often, organizations avoid confronting problems because, quite simply, they are hard to solve. In Fatal Illusions, Lucas asserts, "We need every bit of wisdom we can muster to solve many of the problems that we face as we lead people and organizations. Truth is the way to solutions, but truth is often the first causality when a major problem arises" (Lucas 21). We find easy ways out of the problem-solving process by referring to company history or industry practice or denying the very possibility of change. We've all heard someone justify a bad decision or behavior by saying, "But this is the way we've always done it!" or negating positive recommendations for change by espousing, "The boss will never approve that idea!"

Viewing problems as opportunities for change creates a clear appreciation of the issues impacting the workforce and reveals possible steps toward resolution.

Organizations must begin by rethinking how problems in the past were approached and evaluating what was done right and what was done wrong. We can learn a great deal from the words of Albert Einstein, who said, "The significant problems we face cannot be solved at the same level of thinking we were at when we created them." Managers or supervisors operating in a diverse environment have to be responsible for creating an atmosphere where employees are encouraged to find constructive solutions to workplace challenges. Within the structure of a diverse workplace, issues that a manager may unnecessarily perceive as problems often present themselves. Managers must have the flexibility to alter perspectives and view "problems" as newfound "opportunities." Viewing problems as opportunities for change creates a clear appreciation of the issues impacting the workforce and reveals possible steps toward resolution.

The rapid pace of today's business environment requires managers at all levels of the organizational ladder to handle problems and develop the solutions within their immediate work groups. Managers must take on the roles of teacher, problem solver and facilitator. In order to develop a sense of empowerment and understanding, employees should be allowed to roll up their shirt sleeves and work through the issues as a unified group until there is a resolution. Just as we discussed in the Team Building section, managers can benefit from gathering the different cultural perspectives, values and interests of each employee. During the process of problem solving, managers must make it clear to the work team that the blame game should come to an end. Any comments or put-downs alluding to a certain individual being the source of a problem should not be tolerated.

Next, the team must list all possible alternatives and discuss the pros and cons openly until the best alternative is decided. When employees are involved in shaping the answers to problems (rather than being told what to do by the manager), there is a much greater chance that they will actively implement the change.

When confronted with a challenging situation in your work environment, ask yourself these questions before taking action:

- Is this a problem or an opportunity?
- How does the behavior (displayed by our group or an individual) impact the organization?
- What would success look like if certain issues were resolved?
- Am I willing to invest the mental energy to bring about a resolution?
- Do I fully understand how this issue impacts my organization's bottom line?

COMMITMENT

"There are countless ways of achieving greatness, but any road to achieving one's maximum potential must be built on a bedrock of respect for the individual, a commitment to excellence, and a rejection of mediocrity."

— *Buck Rodgers, former baseball player and manager*

We have explored the building blocks necessary to create a strong foundation for diversity awareness education; now let us lay the keystone. Commitment is the keystone in our foundation for diversity. If an organization does not display a visible and consistent commitment to diversity awareness, workers will not implement diversity awareness in their daily activities. Chief executive officers in organizations across the country have long espoused their commitment to fostering an environment conducive to diversity awareness initiatives. Unfortunately, there are many disconnects between verbiage and reality.

To have a true commitment to the philosophy of diversity, CEOs' actions must be congruent with their words. Developing an organizational commitment to diversity is like sweeping stairs; one must start at the top and work down in order to be effective. Unfortunately, many CEOs are attempting to sweep the stairs from the bottom up; they simply don't understand how diversity awareness directly effects them. The actions of certain leaders remind me of a family that has been ordered to undergo counseling; the father has agreed that the rest of the family should go, but he feels no need to be involved. A CEO can be compared to the head of a household. If the head of the household does not become part of the process, the individual's inaction can produce a dysfunctional team.

Developing an organizational commitment to diversity is like sweeping stairs; one must start at the top and work down in order to be effective.

If you are a leader within an organization, your choice is simple: Do you want to be a part of the solution or a part of the problem? A true commitment to diversity awareness education involves sincere recruitment, realistic selection and objective retention. I've given you the building blocks to create a solid foundation for diversity; now it is your job to pick up the spade and mortar and go to work on putting the pieces together to form your own foundation. As you set out on this meaningful endeavor, here are some final points to ponder:

- Diversity must be...
    o embraced rather than tolerated.
    o woven into every fabric of the organization's culture.
    o a philosophy of the organization rather than a short-lived program.
- Managers and supervisors must be walking billboards for the company's diversity initiatives.
- An organization's vision and mission statements must be congruent with the real work environment.

When the components of diversity are understood, even the toughest cynics can come to realize that it is not a dangerous threat developed to limit organizational success or topple the established power structure. When properly embraced, diversity opens up previously unseen avenues for self-enhancement, increased worker productivity and corporate growth. The companies that will succeed in the 21st century will be the ones that welcome inclusion from various minority groups. One also must remember that a strong diversity program cannot be implemented overnight; there must be a commitment on the part of both the management and the staff.

View the workforce around you not based on their similarities but on the differences they can contribute.

Building a diverse workplace is akin to building a great cathedral; many hearts, hands and heads are involved in the construction and contribute varying skills, all of which are equally important. View the workforce around you not based on their similarities but on the differences they can contribute. A master stonemason cannot complete a cathedral on his own; he needs to focus the efforts of a diverse group of talent in order to achieve the dazzling rainbow of the stained glass windows, the fine workmanship of carved wooden pews or the delicate expressions of carved stone angels. You must act as the master stonemason of your organizational team. Provide them with a solid foundation, and seek ways to unlock their special contributions. So as you lay your first building block, remember that the process toward diversity may not always be easy but that the reward is sublime.

Works Cited

"Are you wasting seven weeks a year?" <u>San Francisco Examiner</u>, Section J-1,13 September 1998:

Giblin, Les. <u>How to Have Confidence and Power in Dealing with People</u>. Englewood Cliffs, New Jersey: Prentice-Hall, Inc., 1956.

Levin, James, and John M. Shanken-Kaye. <u>The Self-Control Classroom: Understanding and Managing the Disruptive Behavior of All Students Including Students with ADHD</u>. Dubuque, Iowa: Kendall/Hunt Publishing Company, 1996.

Lucas, James, R. <u>Fatal Illusions: Shedding a Dozen Unrealities That Can Keep Your Organization From Success</u>. New York: AMACOM American Management Association, 1997.

Nightingale, Earl. <u>The Essence of Success: The Earl Nightingale Library.</u> Your Path to Extraordinary Achievement. Nightingale-Connant, Magazine W180R, n.d.

Tatum, Beverly Daniel. <u>Why Are All the Black Kids Sitting Together in the Cafeteria? And Other Conversations About Race: A Psychologist Explains the Development of Racial Identity</u>. New York: Basic Books, 5th ed., 2003.

Watson, Thomas, S., Jr. <u>Connecting People: Discovering Peace and Power through Cultural Flexibility</u>. Ed. Lawrence W. Watson. Washington, D.C.: Nuff Publications, 1994.

Weiss, Alan. <u>Rejoicing in Diversity</u>. Las Brisas Research Press, 2nd ed. 1994

Benjamin F. Brooks, BA

Ben Brooks empowers individuals, teams and organizations to achieve more effective work teams in a diverse environment. As a retired Major with the Pennsylvania State Police, , with three decades of experience, he has a keen awareness of sensitive workplace issues. Through personal anecdotes, humor, charm, passion and his highly energized, interactive style, Ben is able to immediately connect with his audience on the most serious message. Having lived the experiences he shares with his audiences makes him in demand as a speaker at associations, conferences and organizations. With a Bachelors degree from Kutztown University, a graduate of The FBI National Academy, and thirty years of Law enforcement experience, he brings expertise and strategies that incorporates theory and practice. Ben's topics include: valuing and managing diversity, The Prevention of sexual harassment in the workplace, Conflict resolution, Five keys to effective leadership, and effective communication. His training sessions are conducted in an interactive, participatory, lecturette style, utilizing many popular assessments including the DISC profiles. His clients range from Microsoft Unysis, The city of Philadelphia, The Pennsylvania State Police, Millersville University, Pennsylvania State University, Vassar College, U.S. Department of Agriculture, Dominos Pizza, and Manage Health Network. He is a member of The National Speakers Association.

Benjamin F. Brooks, BA
Major Ben's Consulting Agency
761 Wisteria Way
Collegeville, Pennsylvania 19426
Tel. 1-877-262-1894 (610-409-0214)
Fax: 610-409-8902
E-mail: majorben@comcast.net
www.majorben.speaks4u.com

Chapter Five

Outplacement Services:
Low Risk With High Value

Les Lunceford

Whether downsizing, closing an entire facility or replacing a single manager or executive, outplacement services can help protect employers while significantly assisting separated employees and those left behind.

In this chapter, we will examine some pertinent questions regarding this important subject:

- What is outplacement?
- Is outplacement really worth the trouble?
- What are the advantages for the human resources leader?
- Does outplacement make a difference for the employees, the employer and those left behind?

We should begin, however, with a definition of what outplacement professionals provide:

Outplacement firms deliver individualized and group attention through layoff services—i.e. training, counseling and job development—that focus on the effective job searches for the employees, their families' well-being and their overall careers.

When asked to explain what an outplacement firm does to benefit exiting employees, I usually share a scene I witnessed one day in the gate area of an airport. As I looked out the huge windows of the waiting area to the ground below, I observed a blind man and his guide dog getting off an airplane. Between the plane and the doors of the terminal there were numerous distractions—the roar of the airplane engines, tow motors, baggage handlers and fuel trucks. Despite the many opportunities for distraction, that German shepherd never lost his focus and easily got his master into the safety of the gate area. As the two of them entered a very congested waiting area, more distractions presented themselves, including a small child who tried to pet the dog and French fries on the floor. The guide dog continued his stride by completely ignoring the hectic crowd, the playful child and the savory fries. Within a few minutes, the dog had ushered his master safely to his next gate. As I watched them go through the gate and toward the waiting plane, I couldn't help but think of the role that well-trained and experienced dog played in transitioning his master from a familiar surrounding, through unknown territory and on to his next destination.

Outplacement counselors are like guide dogs. Their objective is to help exiting employees avoid distractions as they journey through a very difficult experience. (They also perform a tremendous service for the employer and retained employees by helping them to avoid distractions or deal with employment issues that are unfamiliar.) Outplacement counselors know the difference between effective job search processes and those that distract from the goal. They know that activity does not equal productivity. They guide others with a focus toward success. A counselor's mission is analogous to that of the guide dog—helping the exiting employee arrive safely at the next destination.

The Wakeup Call

Imagine yourself as an HR professional, sitting in an emergency operations meeting early on Monday morning. The COO has just informed your group that the corporation has done everything it can to control expenses without having to adjust headcount. But here it comes. Before the words are uttered, you know that a significant reduction in labor is next and that you may even be a part of that downsizing.

Are you prepared? Are the managers or division heads prepared for all the eventualities that come with downsizings? Have you been a significant contributor to your operation? Is your job in jeopardy? Are you of the mindset that ignorance is bliss? (In other words, have you been ignorant of business issues affecting the bottom line? As the company's future unfolds, does your ignorance quickly turn into knowledge and bliss into agony?)

At the time of this writing, the nation's unemployment rate is in excess of 6.4 percent, according to the U.S. Labor Department. The number of people on state benefit rolls is now at a two-decade high of almost four million, and in general, the labor market is showing little sign of improvement. The good news is that the economy has been creating jobs—1.5 million over the last year, in fact—from 136.2 million in April 2002 to 137.7 million in April 2003. The problem is that the number of people seeking work is increasing faster than new jobs are being created. And there are literally hundreds of thousands unaccounted for, because they've accepted other temporary or part-time work at wages nowhere near their previous rates.

Many companies have responded to financial, competitive or organizational crises by laying off or terminating employees. And when companies respond, it's always a difficult decision to release employees. High emotions complicate the process and require individualized attention. When the decision is made in any organization to reduce headcount, there are significant issues that could absolutely derail the company's future earnings potential. Consider the effect of a mass layoff relative to continuing production goals, theft and sabotage, violent workplace behavior, increases in accidents and injuries, increases in workers' compensation expenses, employee morale, negative political ramifications, the community's perception, the surviving workforce's attitude, customer base and customer satisfaction, supplier base and shareholder value.

Outplacement Benefits the Employer

Pre Layoff

Some outplacement firms offer strategic-planning assistance to a client company in advance of any major layoff. The client company, which may have little experience in downsizings or closures, may value expert guidance in areas involving labor relations, government mandates, community relations, security, violence and political ramifications.

The proactive outplacement firm will meet with key decision makers as soon as it's practical to obtain necessary background information. At a minimum, the outplacement firm will want to know the product or service, location(s), business rationale for closing, where the work is going because of NAFTA implications, severance benefits, job categories, timing of the event or closure announcement and key organizational objectives.

The outplacement counselors are then able to help management draft the "employee announcement," prepare a script for answering the inevitable barrage of employee questions, communicate with any absent or retired employees who still have vested interests and communicate with customers, suppliers, vendors, community leaders, politicians and any existing union hierarchy.

The questions that employees typically ask of management on the day of a layoff announcement are voluminous:

- When, exactly, will the plant shut down?
- Do we get health care coverage? If so, for how long?
- If I have worked here for fifteen years, what's the size of my severance check? Will there even be a severance check?
- How will I be compensated for my accrued vacation and sick leave?
- Will "bumping" be allowed?
- How will I register for unemployment benefits?
- Is there money available (from the employer or other sources) for retraining?
- What happens to my profit-sharing plan and 401(k)?
- What's NAFTA?
- What's TAA?
- How many others over the age of forty have you laid off?
- Did my performance have anything to do with this layoff?
- If most of us are losing our jobs, how can the company afford to pay bonuses to managers?

Why should a company enlist the strategic-planning services of an outplacement firm? There are numerous value-added opportunities, such as exposure to an outside and objective viewpoint. Focusing on continued productivity, the outplacement firm can help companies avoid:

1. An exodus of workers it needs to maintain production and quality
2. Debilitating morale issues
3. Sabotage or theft
4. OSHA complaints
5. Increases in workers' compensation claims
6. Increases in service expenses
7. Increases in scrap or damaged product

Post Layoff

The value of outplacement is not just in giving an employee a swift escort to the door. Outplacement helps former employees achieve an effective and speedy transition into new roles, i.e. successful placement.

In order to land a new job quickly, the individual must add value to a prospective employer and be positive, motivated and focused on the future instead of dwelling on the past or planning acts of retribution. (Dwelling on the past or thinking of ways to get even evaporates quickly once a person has reason to hope for the future or solidifies his or her life's purpose.)

Left unguided, separated employees may feel unfairly treated, unappreciated, isolated or even trapped. And when personal emotions run high and uncontrolled, the company often sees related problems in three areas: (1) direct costs (2) employee morale and survivor issues and (3) public image.

Direct costs

Hard-dollar savings can be obtained and measured in three main expense areas: unemployment payments, workers' compensation and litigation.

Unemployment

If the employee does not find a job or delays the job search, company-paid unemployment insurance (UI) taxes will be impacted by the benefits charged against the employer's account. This can result in higher-percentage unemployment payroll charges for three years. In many states, an employer's tax rate could be as high as ten percent. In the event of a business sale, merger or acquisition, the UI experience rating may also be acquired.

Workers' Compensation

Employers must avoid the frivolous claims that can consume enormous amounts of time, effort and money. As a result of utilizing outplacement services, companies have documented improvements in safety records and corresponding drops in workers' compensation claims and lawsuits. One Michigan company we assisted left untouched a reserve intended for the sole purpose of workers' compensation claims following a plant closure. There was not even a one percent increase in workers' compensation expenses for the 1,400 affected employees. Fortunately, the company's leadership took proactive measures prior to announcing the facility's closure and had contracted outplacement services. The result was nearly a ten-to-one return on their investment.

Litigation

An employee's job is often a large part of that person's identity. When someone loses a job, a loss of identity ensues. Without emotional support and motivation for job search, a displaced person can become hostile toward the company, dwell on the negatives and feel neglected, unappreciated and betrayed. Litigation is often the outcome. Outplacement bolsters confidence, provides individual coaching and assistance, focuses on opportunities and helps motivate the employee to pursue a successful job search. Some outplacement firms routinely mediate disputes between an employer and the departing employee to resolve any severance issues.

Employee morale and survivor issues

With a downsizing or closure, a company faces real issues of productivity, quality, safety, sabotage and security in addition to the loss of key people.

All too often, companies make the decision to reduce headcount, but it's not until after the announcement that they realize the need to fill the pipeline with product and build an inventory. During this time, production and other demands on the workforce increase. Individuals (knowing they are about to lose their jobs) may be required to work more overtime and turn out more products than at any other time in their career.

Employee morale is critical to customer satisfaction during the transitional time. Frequently, companies that offer professional outplacement services actually experience improved employee morale, production goals are achieved, if not over-achieved, and a high quality of work is accomplished. In addition, the morale of the remaining employees is crucial. They are watching closely to see how their peers and friends are being treated.

Public image

What value does your company put on community perception? Rumors can run rampant during times of change, but a company's good reputation can be preserved if it deals with employees in a fair and compassionate manner.

Many companies spend a great deal of money on charities, schools and local associations to build a positive image as good corporate citizens in their communities. Companies cannot risk a negative impact on business, be it related to current or future customers. The impact on stockholders, media, politicians and even competitors must also be considered.

Outplacement Benefits the Retained Employees

Remaining individuals have concerns about the future of the company, its stability, their own personal growth and whether or not such layoffs might affect them in the future as well. Lack of loyalty, confusion, anger, distrust, increased stress, frustration and resentment are all serious surviving-employee issues. By minimizing individual and work-family stress, preserving dignity and communicating directly with all concerned, a company can enhance the morale of employees being displaced as well as those being retained. The outplacement firm can advise the company on ways to support its retained employees or survivors.

When downsizing occurs, attention naturally focuses on those who have lost their jobs. But layoffs can have a significant impact on the remaining workforce. Those who are left behind often suffer anxiety, depression, betrayal and feelings of guilt. Management continues to have high expectations for the workforce to maintain or even increase its workload and continue loyal behavior.

Many who survive worry about the "next round." They put their lives on hold, delaying the purchase of a home, car, a child's braces or elective medical treatment until a time when, they hope, the upheaval has ended.

When cutbacks occur, workflow, quality, safety and relationships are affected. Managers struggle to meet company commitments with the remaining workforce, only to find an increase in job-performance problems, because productivity declines when employees are stressed and uneasy.

Many have developed long-time friendships with co-workers who were laid off. Some even feel tremendous guilt that they are still employed while their friends are on the street. Often, those who were laid off are provided outplacement services, severance and extended benefits. They get to move on with their lives—even start with a clean slate. This isn't the case with survivors.

Remaining workers may come down with Layoff Survivor Disorder (LSD). Symptoms include job insecurity, stress from increased workloads, resistance to change, decreased loyalty and commitment, unwillingness to go beyond the minimum and complete loss of confidence in the management team.

What can a company's leadership do to control LSD?

1. Have a well-designed layoff process. A good overall process won't necessarily cure LSD, but it will help prevent survivors from becoming overly discouraged.

    a. Make the reductions clear and quick.

    b. Develop and maintain upward, downward and lateral communication networks that can be used openly and frequently. Bad information or false rumors can demoralize the entire workforce.

    c. Provide prior notice. Be certain to abide by any federal and/or state laws, such as the Worker Adjustment and Retraining Act (WARN), which requires sixty-day notices in certain situations.

    d. Be fair and explain decisions openly.

2. Give survivors time to grieve. Even when a layoff is expertly managed, the remaining workforce may still feel vulnerable and violated. Establishing support groups is an effective means of bringing emotions out in the open. In a very short period of time, departments or work teams can make significant progress in unblocking and managing anxiety.

3. Make an all-out effort to help employees become more productive. Improve job design, provide better tools and remove barriers that impede a person's ability to do a good job. This is definitely a time to evaluate processes and streamline to avoid unnecessary work.

4. Increase training expenditures. After a major reorganization, building new teams is essential to establishing relationships that will ultimately increase productivity. When management participates in effective team-building activities, confidence can be restored at all levels.

5. Encourage people to manage their own careers instead of relying on the organization to call all the shots. Today's working environment requires employees to develop transferable skills and have a certain level of independence from their employers. By cross training and seeking more responsibilities, employees make themselves more valuable to their employers while at the same time strengthening their own careers. Additionally, when employees perceive an increase in their individual worth, they feel less victimized and more in control of their own fates.

6. Since rapid technological change requires a willingness to adapt and learn, encourage people to adopt a mindset of lifelong learning. The old behavior was: In youth, we learn; in adulthood, we earn; in later years, we retire. Today's model of behavior is more complex: In youth, we prepare for a lifetime of learning; in young adulthood, we vocationally learn and earn; and in adulthood, we earn, re-learn and possibly even retire. In late adulthood, more retire, earn a little less and learn to keep up with a fast-paced world.

7. Make more time to listen to employees. Timely, truthful and sincere communication with all workers is the key to alleviating tension and anxiety. Often, employees are not looking for specific answers, but simply an opportunity to be heard. If you make time to listen, be sure it is quality time free from distractions.

8. Never, ever underestimate the value of basic leadership and recognition. This essential principle is so crucial that it deserves

special attention. Managers must be more than just good business people. Some of the leadership qualities that successful companies embrace really have nothing to do with the business world. They have more to do with passion and energy combined with the ability to positively influence others.

Recognizing and praising individuals for a job well done is an example of this type of encouragement. Managers and supervisors who are passionate about their co-workers and positively influence them are models of excellence.

How do you improve your ability to influence others? As a leader, you have to serve others and subordinate personal needs to those of your team members.

Sometimes leaders think only of their own careers or personal gain, thus allowing egos to cloud their judgment. When this occurs, they lose sight of the team's needs. They fail to understand that the strength of an organization depends on leaders who first are concerned with doing what's best for their followers and then show appreciation for the individual efforts and achievements that helped the team accomplish its goals.

Recognition and praise for a job well done are two of the most effective but underutilized leadership tools at your disposal. According to makeup magnate Mary Kay Ash, "The only things that people want more than sex and money are recognition and praise."

Recognition also builds healthy working relationships, especially among those who have survived a major layoff. Labor unrest, high turnover, strikes, etc. are all symptoms of a management-employee relationship problem. The legitimate needs of the workforce aren't being met. Look for the root cause of unrest and you'll find an opportunity to improve relationships.

When managers focus only on the tasks at hand and not on relationships, it often will lead to excessive employee turnover, poor quality production, low levels of loyalty and commitment, lack of trust and even rebellion. But through development of healthy relationships and attention to employees' needs, most of these turbulent situations can be avoided.

People never outgrow their need for recognition, praise or yearning for acceptance. Successful leaders combine a healthy dose of fun with appreciation to create a positive work environment. A supervisor who reinforces achievements with humorous, memorable acts of recognition will experience a winning combination—a work environment that empowers, motivates and is downright fun. Life is too short to be ordinary. A light-hearted event at work can dissolve daily tension.

Acknowledging and meeting employees' needs can unleash a source of creativity, energy and enthusiasm that turns problems into opportunities and achievements. What is recognized is reinforced, and what is reinforced is repeated. If you want to improve attendance or safety at work, reward excellent performance and encourage good habits.

Some may think that laughter, fun and play are not appropriate in a professional environment. Nothing could be further from the truth. These things have been relieving stress for thousands of years. Some 2,500 years ago, the Greek philosopher Herodotus recognized the danger in taking ourselves too seriously: "If a man insisted always on being serious, and never allowed himself a bit of fun and relaxation, he would surely go mad or become unstable without knowing it."

Job stress is one of today's leading causes of illness. An early indicator of mental fatigue is the loss of joy in being alive. Appropriate humor in the workplace is vital and sometimes critical for human survival.

Emotional Concerns and Life's Disappointments

Cost cutting and restructuring have taken a heavy toll on the job market. As a human resources professional, it's crucial that you understand the emotional reactions of being laid off. Being laid off can be one of life's enormous disappointments. And every day (regardless of the economy), thousands of people are experiencing the loss of a job.

If you have ever been downsized (or whatever expression you choose to describe losing a job), I am here to tell you that you can actually thrive from the experience.

When my two sisters and I were younger, I learned from watching my mother agonize over losing her manufacturing job. This was a particularly difficult period in her life since she was caring for three children without our father. She regularly worried over which bills to pay and which ones to let slide.

As her self-esteem slowly recovered, she realized that she was not overly fond of the job anyway and, in fact, dreamed of becoming a nurse. Her downsizing and subsequent turmoil gave her an opportunity to fulfill her calling. With a great amount of perseverance and some state funding, she made a leap of faith with grace and accomplished her goal of entering the nursing profession. She thrived as a nurse for the next twenty-five years and successfully raised her three children. Ironically, had it not been for her job loss, she may never have realized her dream of becoming a nurse.

Mindset of Departing Employees and the Role of Outplacement Counselors

The following information and suggestions will help you as a human resources professional to understand the mindset of the departing employees and the role of outplacement firms. Some of these suggestions are common sense, although common sense frequently becomes uncommon during periods of turmoil.

In today's job market, there is no such thing as job security. And no matter what economic conditions prevail, no one owes anyone a job. There are no more gold watch awards at the conclusion of a thirty-year career in corporate America. Because of this, employees should work at honing their skills and abilities and aggressively market their value. (Learning how and actually marketing a person's skills and abilities is part of an outplacement counselor's mission.)

Outplacement (OP) counselors encourage employees not to allow emotions to get in the way of progress and reduce their ability to survive during career transitions. Being laid off and searching for a new job can cause severe emotional trauma. Many rate job loss as a shock equal to divorce or losing a loved one. Such trauma can trigger a sequence of emotions that create dysfunction for the task at hand.

Turmoil can drain energy and enthusiasm from search activities, magnify problems beyond their importance, create distortion in other areas like personal relationships and family life, focus excessive attention on side issues and just annihilate self-esteem.

Generally, the emotions of a laid-off individual appear in the following sequence:

1. **Denial**. Here, the focus is on having or making the responsible people correct their "mistake" rather than on finding another job. Those who are laid off reason, "They made a mistake," "If I can just talk to them..." "When they take another look at this, the whole thing will change" or "They can't do this; they owe me."

2. **Betrayal**. As time passes and it becomes clear that the decision will stand, the denial phase is replaced by feelings of betrayal, a violation of trust and a sense of abandonment. Anger can set in

and harden. A yearning to "get even with the bastards" can take hold.

3. **Fear**. Out of betrayal emerge fear and even more anger. There is fear of an uncertain future, embarrassment occasioned by having to look for work and anger at whoever was responsible for putting the employee in this situation. Getting even is self-destructive behavior and should not be an option. Fear and anger (both difficult to disguise) will make the person much less attractive to another employer and will certainly sabotage job-search activities.

4. **Guilt**. Feelings of guilt may emerge. People begin to wonder if there were things they could have done to avoid the layoff. People may become plagued with self-doubt and second thoughts about their actions.

5. **Depression**. At this stage, the person may become discouraged and drained of energy and motivation. Delays and a lengthy screening process associated with filling job vacancies feed on guilt and self-doubt. Some will carry more emotional baggage than others. The important thing for them is to recognize it, deal with it and not let it interfere with their efforts.

When individuals are laid off and you observe discouragement, consider it normal behavior. People should acknowledge those feelings, discuss them and then consciously put them aside. Many, however, can't just put their feelings aside, and they slip back into feelings of guilt, anger and depression. This may happen when the person goes to her mailbox and discovers one rejection letter after another or when certain employers refuse to return telephone calls. OP counseling and processes that accompany counseling sessions are very effective in helping individuals navigate through such periods of discouragement.

OP professionals will encourage a person to get started with the job search as soon as possible. An individual with a mindset centered on a solution to a problem is less troubled by the problem. If employees are fortunate enough to have severance packages that include OP, however, they shouldn't think of it as a big cushion. When a potential employer asks, "What have you been doing since your layoff?" the expected reply should not be, "Hunting wild boar" or "Fly fishing for trout." By the way, no reputable outplacement firm would ever encourage a job candidate to exhaust all severance benefits before seriously searching for work.

Finding a job is a job in itself. Affected individuals should schedule their time so they have an active and organized search, but not so active it results in burnout or major stress. The keys to an effective job search are realistic goals, self-confidence, skills and abilities, and a solid job-search process. And it is paramount for job hunters to widen their scope by recognizing other opportunities.

Activity vs. Productivity

Another reason for turning to outside experts is that many unemployed people "don't know they don't know." That is, a person can literally waste time, energy and money doing things that yield absolutely no return on his or her investment.

Activity simply does not equal productivity. The sinkhole that people often fall into when they have a huge list of things to do (or prospective employers to contact) is thinking that the only answer is to work longer and harder. And so the frenzy begins. People can often be at their busiest when their productivity is at its lowest.

Put another way, working or prospecting for new job opportunities in a frenzied state adds a lot more stress to the process, and it takes people longer to accomplish their goal of landing new employment.

Certain amounts of stress are healthy and add a sense of urgency to the overall process. But too much stress can push people to a level that causes productivity to plummet. Think of the ocean where the surface is choppy but there are gentle swells below. Working at a pace where we are tossed back and forth by the surface waves is not conducive to productivity, and it is certainly not good for our overall well-being.

By encouraging displaced workers to plan their efforts, OP professionals help them look at all the contingencies and best available alternatives. This means a greater likelihood of getting the job done right in the first place, which is finding the right job to fit their needs. With proper planning and proven processes, activity can equal productivity, and the employee can focus on doing the right thing, as opposed to just doing things right.

Outplacement Firms Can Ease the Resistance

Do people resist change? If you responded positively—then you're mostly wrong! What people resist, technically, is the transition. The less difficult the transition, the less resistance there is to change.

Think about the last time you participated in a major change at work. The more management communicated with you, solicited your advice and provided processes, structure and leadership, the easier the transition. All are equally essential resources for bringing about effective change.

Whether you're involved in a work project or you're assisting employees being laid off from work, people need processes, structure and leadership to navigate their transition. The loss of a job leads to a challenge that will never be forgotten. Without the appropriate resources, the transition is a significant obstacle.

The reason so many people have such a difficult time with job loss is that they have not been afforded the overall support and counseling it takes to weather the storm. With no support (in terms of processes, structure and leadership) they may resent their employers, often to the point of trying to get even with them. If a soon-to-be unemployed worker has an entitlement mentality, someone else (the employer) is likely to pay a high cost for the employee's job loss.

As an HR professional or senior manager, you're inviting hostility and perhaps even litigation if you allow your top decision makers to ignore the workforce once they've delivered the bad news. Adding a disgruntled spouse or an aggressive union to the mix may only compound matters. Ignoring the workforce during a downsizing makes you a target for disgruntled plaintiffs.

Laid off individuals who have the most difficulty finding meaningful employment are those who don't have a clue about what it takes to acquire a new job during a sluggish economy. These people are those who "don't know they don't know." They need processes, structure and leadership just as much as they did within their previous work teams. With millions of unemployed people looking for limited work opportunities, the uneducated and unsupported people are going to be like most of the pack and take many months to find a job. Even if they do find employment quickly, it may not be the right fit; the new job could be just a "port in a storm." Without using proper methods or processes, they could easily find themselves in the job market again in a short period of time. Unfortunately, they'll now have to explain to the next prospective employer why they were laid off in the first place and then why the most recent job opportunity didn't materialize.

Here's an unfortunate example of how one individual manager was at a total loss when he lost his position with a major insurance company in the Northeast. He fit into that "don't know they don't know" category previously mentioned.

I came across the gentleman's photo in a major business publication. Dressed professionally and standing on a busy street corner, he was holding a sign for the entire world to see that read, "Insurance professional needs work. Call XXX-XXXX (his home number)." The business article communicated a story of personal desperation, and it inspired me to contact him.

I gave the gentleman a call to find out how he had landed in such a predicament. I learned that he had been out of work for over a year, had no viable opportunities, was over the age of fifty and his severance benefits and unemployment compensation were completely exhausted. He was down to his last few dollars in savings, and he was beginning to live off his 401(k). He was now without healthcare benefits, and his wife, who hadn't worked for years, had health issues. What I heard was not shocking, given the fact that he'd never been afforded outplacement assistance or even counseling from his former employer. He was bitter, wanted to get even and mentioned the term "age discrimination" on at least two occasions.

Within minutes of introducing myself to this gentleman, I quickly figured that he didn't have a clue as to what he should have been doing during the previous year. He admitted to seeing signs of an impending layoff years before the event. Had he behaved proactively? No. He had hoped it wouldn't happen to him. He had figured that hope was a strategy, and now he was learning it was not. (It's perfectly fine to hope or to pray, but keep rowing for the shore at the same time).

By the time his photo and story appeared in the paper, he had mailed out hundreds of resumes with no success. Here's what he shared with me:

1. Over the previous year, he'd mailed over 700 resumes, most without a cover letter, to recipients who weren't really expecting them. This was a significant waste of time, stationary, stamps, etc. Resumes should arrive "warm"; that is, as the result of a telephone conversation, a personal meeting or successful networking with others.

2. His self-esteem had taken a direct hit. I was hearing a man who had been whittled down to a mere twig of his previous existence. Had I (or anyone else accustomed to telephone screening job candidates) been speaking with him regarding employment opportunities, his demeanor and tone of voice would have immediately turned me off. What employer wants to hire an insurance executive with little or no self-esteem? None.

3. He whined about the lack of notice and very little severance. He was still belaboring the past. (Another waste of time; we can't change the past.) He had no solid network of friends, associates or former bosses in which he could confide.

4. He only started to network when he got into trouble. (Strengthening a personal network is an ongoing process. It can't be initiated successfully the day one loses his or her job.)

5. I could go on, but to add insult to injury (and to his self-esteem) some passersby had actually shouted insults and vulgarities at the man and on one occasion had even thrown beer bottles at him.

As a former VP of HR in a major corporation, I have screened thousands of resumes and cover letters, initially spending just moments on each one. If my name was spelled wrong, it showed a lack of attention to detail and was all the excuse I needed to decrease my workload by pitching the resume in the trash. If the cover letter went on and on and sounded like it came straight from a book, it was tossed. If a resume was full of fluff (no quantifiable results or substance that demonstrated value), it was another easy pitch. If the overall appearance was not professional looking, it landed in the trash. Misspelled words or grammatical errors throughout the resume or cover letter also resulted in rejection. (Again, I was looking for attention to detail. With the advent of spell check software, there's no excuse for such mistakes in a document that's so important.)

The unfortunate subject on the other end of the telephone had never heard of the things I have just pointed out. He actually thought I was being too critical of job applicants. Again, he fell into the "don't know they don't know" grouping. Had outplacement counseling been made available to him, he would have known better and would more than likely have been working instead of standing on a street corner pleading for an opportunity and contemplating an age discrimination complaint with the EEOC.

By the way, a reputable outplacement firm is cheaper than a bad one. Exercise due diligence when selecting outplacement firms; don't choose on price alone. Know whom you're dealing with and know their reputation. Check with previous client companies and other references, go visit their offices and check out the support afforded to the individual executive or the group of employees. Can they deliver on their promises? Do they under deliver or do they have a reputation of over delivering?

What Must Human Resource Professionals Do?

As a part of management, you can help employees by providing guidance and support before they exit the premises. Help them maintain a strong sense of self-worth by consciously holding on to their strengths and accomplishments in order to offset self-doubt. Job searches create frustration and rejection (both real and imagined) for the strongest of individuals. It is important that feelings be put into perspective vis-à-vis years of accomplishment and transferable skills.

Help employees stay upbeat. Affected persons should remind themselves of their goal to turn the situation into something positive. Help them explore all viable options, but be particularly aggressive in those areas that might enrich the quality of their lives.

If employees can maintain self-worth and remain upbeat, the transition should go more smoothly, and perhaps some roadblocks will be reduced to mere speed bumps. Said another way, obstacles can be turned into opportunities.

At the minimum, outplacement assistance should:

1. Provide information to the management team to assist it through the planning stages as well as the transitional phases. Some managers may or may not have experienced the challenges and frustrations associated with layoffs and, in either case, may welcome expert guidance.

2. Make information regarding planned actions, such as severance payments and extension of benefits, available to affected employees.

3. Offer group training and one-on-one counseling with affected employees concerning the entire job search process.

4. Publish announcements to other employers (local and nationwide) regarding the availability of qualified employees.

5. Assist in developing cover letters and resumes for each affected employee to be sent to potential employers.

6. Coach individuals on telephone skills, networking, interviewing, salary negotiations and running an organized job search.

7. Facilitate life-and career-planning workshops, which help people fully understand their career goals and to cope with the major emotional changes accompanying job loss. Additional workshops may also cover financial planning, starting and managing a small business, and retirement planning.

The advantages of outplacement services are clear—a severance benefit that helps departing employees identify and evaluate their options and then assists them in achieving their targeted goal, which is usually finding new employment. Equally important, outplacement services can help employers avoid obvious and hidden costs, improve existing employee morale, maintain good community relations, and satisfy the customer. These incentives alone can justify the use of outplacement services.

Les Lunceford

Les Lunceford is the Chief Executive Officer of The Alliance of Tennessee Employers, Inc. and President of The Transition Team – Knoxville. Prior to co-founding the Alliance and joining The Transition Team (an international Human Resources consulting firm specializing in group and individual outplacement) he was the Vice President of Human Resources for a $1.7 billion NYSE firm. His strengths include strategic organizational development, start-up operations, leadership, teambuilding and workforce reductions. Les was a career U.S. Marine Corps officer and a veteran of the Persian Gulf War. He's listed on a national speaker's bureau and lectures nationwide on the subject of leadership. He has co-authored a book on career transitions and is a contributing author for career advice in a major metropolitan newspaper. His knowledge of the winning principles of leadership and interpersonal communications is extensive. Through his participatory presentations, he has inspired and refocused all levels of management on the essential elements of successful leadership. He has a B.S. degree in Political Science and Business from East Tennessee State University in Johnson City, Tennessee.

Les Lunceford
CEO, The Alliance of Tennessee Employers, Inc. &
President, The Transition Team - Knoxville
9111 Cross Park Drive, Suite A-250
Knoxville, TN 37923
865.694.3848
LLunceford@atedirect.com
LLunceford@transitionteam.com
www.atedirect.com
www.transitionteam.com

Chapter Six

Learning—It's Everybody's Business

Therese M. Malm, MA

This chapter contains helpful and application-ready information for individuals and organizations who desire a learning-the-business environment and wish to embed this concept into their organization's culture.

What do I mean by a "learning-the-business" environment? Let me ask you three questions:

1. Are you, or is your organization interested in making more money because of a direct link between your work force and business results such as profits and customer satisfaction?

2. Are you, or is your organization interested in a work force that is responsible and accountable for having a full and complete understanding of the business as well as how it can positively impact the bottom line?

3. Are you, or is your organization committed to linking people systems (staffing, compensation, performance management, training and development, employee relations) with common behavioral indicators (competencies) that are aligned with business vision, core values, strategy, operational goals and individual employee goals?

If you answered yes to these questions, then you are interested in a learning-the-business environment, and you will definitely benefit from implementing the ideas and recommendations found in this chapter.

For reference sake, the definition of "Learning –It's Everybody's Business" is straightforward. It is an environment that can demonstrate a direct link between the work force and business results. This link is fully and completely understood by each individual in the organization. Each individual is responsible and accountable for learning the business. "Learning—It's Everybody's Business" can be tailored to your needs and customized as you see fit. This information can be useful, whether you are a consultant, a manager, an HR staff member or an individual contributor.

It cannot be unleashed without a vision and the willingness of an individual (or group of individuals) who will not settle for anything less and insist on being first past the post.

I have consulted with various organizations, both public and private, profit and not-for-profit, and learning the business is a powerful and alluring call to every individual within an organization. It cannot be unleashed without a vision and the willingness of an individual (or group of individuals) who will not settle for anything less and insist on being first past the post. I encourage you to read on and take the necessary steps to deliver on this initiative for your organization.

Learning—It's Everybody's Business. Says Who?

Life experience—that's who! Take a hard and honest look at how essential it is for you to remain in a continuous state of learning, to stay current and, in most cases, stay ahead of the game just to keep some semblance of order and balance in your daily life. If you fail to stay current with changes in technology, health, the service industry or education, to name a few, you may find yourself in some tough and frustrating circumstances. You may be unable to make a call from a pay phone; you may gain weight while trying to lose weight because you are carbo loading but sedentary; you may not be able to get money from your bank account on a day the bank is closed because you refuse to use an ATM card; you will pay an extra $75 for an airline ticket because you aren't sure how to get an e-ticket; you may stand in line an extra fifteen minutes because you aren't sure how to use the self-check-out line in your favorite grocery store; you will be unable to buy a book for forty percent less than retail or earn continuing education credits from an online course because you do not have a computer, e-mail address or an Internet Service Provider. Do you need any more proof? These examples demonstrate that you need to be in a state of continuous learning in all aspects of life, or it gets real expensive, real fast. It costs in terms of your money, your time, your energy and your experience.

I challenge every organization to go another step further and focus on what the world's greatest work forces do differently. They aggressively adopt the mindset that learning is everybody's business.

It's hard to dispute the fact that learning is everybody's business. Truth be told, this applies to all of life, in and outside of the workplace. But more than ever, there is a tremendous expectation in the workplace that each person have a working knowledge and broad understanding of the business that is far beyond and more in-depth than the completion of daily job tasks. Learning the business is now a matter of business and a matter of fact. People are truly having a direct impact on business outcomes. There is now a direct link between people and the bottom line. How well a work force makes it its business to learn the business is directly linked to a broad range of business results—customer satisfaction, retention (of both high performers and customers), productivity and profits. Marcus Buckingham and Curt Coffman, authors of *First, Break All The Rules*, refer to a work force that has learned the business and has a direct impact on the bottom line. A key focus of the authors' research reveals what the world's greatest managers do differently.

I challenge every organization to go another step further and focus on what the world's greatest work forces do differently. They aggressively adopt the mindset that learning is everybody's business. As quoted in *First Break All The Rules*, Jack Welch, former CEO of General Electric, said, "Any company trying to compete must figure out a way to engage the mind of every employee." For the purposes of this chapter, the term "engaged employee" translates into a learning-the-business mindset. That fact is now indisputable; it is supported by extensive research and proof that an engaged work force gives you the competitive edge and helps you make money through the business measures of productivity, customer satisfaction, profitability and retention.

The "Learning—It's Everybody's Business" Environment

So what exactly is learning the business comprised of? What does it mean? What does it look like in the work place? Several components are visible and evident in a work environment in which learning is everybody's business.

Alignment of the Vision, Business Strategy and Core Values

In this environment, the vision is alive and well understood, not just a framed fixture hanging on a hallway wall. Core values are thoughtfully determined and fully integrated into the company's expectations of employees throughout company communications. (Every memo, company e-mail, intranet site, Internet site, state-of-the-business address, letterhead and newsletter must carry a consistent message.) Business strategy is incorporated into day-in-day-out operational plans from business units to individual goals; that is, every people system—staffing, compensation, performance management, etc.—must use the same measurements.

Each employee truly gets it. Each employee understands that he is responsible and accountable for learning the business, and the company fully supports him with tools and resources.

The strengths of the company and each individual are known and understood. Customers, competitors, distributors, suppliers and vendors—basically, any business relationship with or within the company understands and knows the company vision, core values and business strategy. This alignment means that everybody has the access and knowledge to be on the same page and to clearly understand the roles and strengths they possess to play a big part in helping the business succeed. Each employee truly gets it. Each employee understands that he is responsible and accountable for learning the business, and the company fully supports him with tools and resources.

It takes time, energy, focus, belief and perseverance on the part of key leadership for alignment to occur and remain intact for the long term. The rest of the work force will follow the leadership example. If you are part of a company that isn't quite there but is at least doing its very best to get there, then you have a good chance of achieving alignment. You will simply have more obstacles to deal with along the way.

Linking of People Systems

In this environment, human resources has a make-it-or-break-it role. HR executes a full and complete linking of every one of its systems and ensures that there are no gaps or weak links that could put the entire environment at risk. Each people system (staffing, performance management, compensation, employee relations, organization development, training, etc.) is linked directly to the vision statement, core values, strategic plan, and operational and individual goals through behavior indicators. (Behavior indicators are the visible and concrete actions that can be measured and are evident in the way people think, talk and act each day at work. Companies refer to these behaviors as competencies, values or performance criteria). Each employee participates by having a full command of the behavior indicators (competencies) related to his position. With this knowledge he is responsible for writing behavior-related goals, with coaching from his manager.

In this environment, human resources has a make-it-or-break-it role. HR executes a full and complete linking of every one of its systems and ensures that there are no gaps or weak links that could put the entire environment at risk.

The goals are written in alignment with operational goals, core values and business strategy. Each goal has a measurement that links it directly to a business result, such as retention, customer satisfaction, productivity and profits. The behavior indicators serve as the common and essential denominator that the people systems use to measure goal alignment. When a company uses the same criteria for hiring as it does to develop, train, manage performance and reward high performance, then its people systems are linked with the behavior indicators that are aligned with the individual goals, business goals,

109

strategy, core values and the vision statement. This alignment makes it possible for the human resources of a company to be tied directly to bottom-line results.

When people systems are linked with behavior indicators (competencies), then the primary focus of each and every person employed by that organization is "how" they do their job tasks, not "what" their job tasks are. This coincides with the adage that it's not "what" happens to you that matters but "how" you handle it or respond. If the work force primarily operates with the mindset of "how" to do a job, then this mindset takes the company up a notch to another level of performance. Thinking about "how" to work means that a work force is fully engaged and committed to learning the business.

Thinking about "how" to work means that a work force is
fully engaged and committed to learning the business.

Thinking about the "what" means that your work force has a job/task mentality. It will perform and get the job done, but you won't be able to link the completion of tasks alone to business results.

Think about the mindset of "how" and the change that can occur in a person's approach to her job day in and day out. This mindset ignites creativity, innovation, business savvy, synergy, awareness and inspirational leadership within an organization. If the majority of your work force walks through the door in the morning and just does the tasks of its jobs, you are at risk of having just a recreational work force. If the majority of your work force walks through the door in the morning and thinks about "how" to do its jobs and "how" it will respond to each and every situation, then you've got an expert and proficient work force in an active and conscious state of learning the business. Forefront in the mind of such a work force are retention of customers, global competitiveness, customer satisfaction, productivity and making money. Individuals in this type of work force know and understand company vision, strategies, core values, operational goals, their own goals and how these business components relate to their jobs. They take all of these components into consideration when performing job tasks. This combination keeps them focused on the "how"—how to increase retention, profits, productivity and customer satisfaction. It does not matter what position a person holds, she has to be continuously focused on the "how" and the response, not just the job tasks. Only then can a business show a direct link between people and business results that positively impact the bottom line.

Consider this example of the "how" versus the "what" in a very common work situation.

The "What"

A call is received by a CSR, who answers the phone and offers assistance. The customer is irate because of an incorrect late fee charge. The CSR conveys to the customer that the billing is correct and that the customer is misunderstanding the billing. The CSR further states that the late charge will stand. He asks the customer if she understands. The customer pleads with the CSR and asks for an exception since she has had such a good history with the company. On average, she purchases $2,500 per month. At times, she has carried a balance and had to pay interest, but her payments have been on time for the past seven years. The CSR acknowledges her good standing but again stands his ground and asks for her understanding. Because she understands her error, she acquiesces and lets the CSR know that she understands. The call ends. The CSR tracks the call, noting the issues and that it has been resolved. The company will get the late charge fee of $35 from the customer.

On the other end, the customer writes out a check to the credit card company for the amount of purchases plus the late fee. She then takes a pair of scissors from her drawer, cuts the card in two and throws the pieces into the garbage. She looks in her purse and takes out a credit card for which she has just received approval and places it behind her ATM card, the place where she used to place the credit card that she just threw away. The new card is easily accessible, and she knows she will be using it extensively during this holiday season; she anticipates about $4,500 in purchases. Her phone rings; it is a friend of hers calling about going shopping. Before setting up the details of the shopping trip, she tells her friend about the horrible and unhelpful customer service she just experienced. She states that all the customer service rep did was repeat the same lines, not listening to her at all. Her friend asks for the name of the company and says that she will be sure to never use a credit card from this company.

The "How"

A call is received by a CSR, who answers the phone and offers assistance. The customer is irate because of an incorrect late fee charge.

The CSR acknowledges that the customer is upset and assures her that he can get her questions answered. (His mindset leads him to consider matters of retention and customer satisfaction.) He conveys to the customer that the billing is correct and that she is misunderstanding the billing. He offers to walk her through what she misunderstands, and she agrees. The CSR acknowledges the customer's long standing with the company and the fact that her payments have been timely for seven years. (His mindset leads him to think about cost versus profit.) He also notes that she purchases, on average, $2,500 per month and at times carries a balance of around $5,000 per month at 11.9 percent APR. He asks her why her payment was late this time. (His mindset leads him to consider productivity and spend the time with her, even though the call may go longer than the call system recommends. But he knows he is going to retain a longtime customer, and is therefore energized.) She explains that it was a simple oversight due to a Monday holiday. He listens and says that he understands how that could happen. He further conveys to the customer that he will make an exception on this month's statement and remove the late fee of $35 immediately. He reviews the balance with her so that she knows the exact amount to write on her check. He asks the customer if she understands everything. She conveys to him that she does and thanks him for how well he handled her situation. She tells him that she will continue to use her card because of his great service. He expresses his appreciation, lets her know that she is a valued customer and thanks her for her years of loyalty. The phone conversation ends. The CSR tracks the issue and resolution, showing a loss of $35, and notes that the customer expressed her intent to remain a customer based on how well he had worked with her. He notes that she is a long-term, high-volume customer.

On the other end, the customer puts her credit card back in its place, where it has been for the last seven years, just behind her ATM card. The card is easily accessible, and she knows she will be using it extensively during the upcoming holiday season; in fact, she anticipates about making about $4,500 in purchases. She writes out her check in the amount that the CSR conveyed to her. Her phone rings; it is a friend of hers calling about going shopping. Before setting up the details of the shopping trip, she tells her friend about the great customer service she just experienced. Her friend confirms this, sharing that it is the only credit card she uses, because anytime she has an issue, the staff always helps her out.

The first scenario describes a CSR completing the tasks of his job. By completing the tasks, he secures the $35 late payment fee for the company, but he has no idea that he has just lost a customer. Retention doesn't even cross his mind. He is doing his job tasks, and he executes each one according to his job description. In the second scenario, the CSR is continuously in the zone of knowing the business. At every junction, he is considering and weighing the consequences of each decision he makes. How will it impact retention, customer satisfaction, production and profit? In the end, $35 is a small cost compared to the retention of this long-term, high-volume customer.

You can see by this example that there is a clear distinction between the "what" and the "how." You can do this with each role in the organization. Many organizations assume that employees will naturally incorporate the "how" into their daily job tasks. Nothing could be further from the truth or reality. A company must constantly bombard and equip the work force with the necessary tools, resources, information and expectations of the "how" so that they become autonomic. The work force mindset of "*What* part of my job do I need to give priority to today?" or "*What* do I need to do before break, lunch or the end of the day?" is narrowly focused and needs to go.

The mindset of "how" leads to a whole different work experience for the individual and completely different results for the business. This mindset focuses on "*How* do I help get better numbers on customer satisfaction, profits and retention?"

As I mentioned earlier in this chapter, there is now substantial, valid and reliable research that demonstrates that the work force can have a direct and positive impact on the bottom line.

> The Gallup Organization research, as described in *First, Break All The Rules*, substantiated the fact that talented employees need great managers. The research produced a model called The Gallup Path to Business Performance. This path shows that when an organization can identify the strengths of its work force, find the right fit and select great managers, then it has a work force that is engaged—a work force that fully participates in, knows and understands the business. The effect is a work force that has a direct positive impact on productivity, retention, profitability and customer loyalty. The business result is customer loyalty, sustainable growth, real profit increase and, finally, a stock increase.

This would be a fatal mistake that an organization pays for with loss of talent, loss of customers, a propensity for selecting and hanging onto poor leaders, a mediocre work environment and, worse yet, bankruptcy.

The evidence is in; employees have a direct impact on how well a business makes money. Corporate decision makers and leaders of vision, values, policies and practices can no longer dismiss this convincing research as trendy "people stuff" or the current flavor of the month. This would be a fatal mistake that an organization pays for with loss of talent, loss of customers, a propensity for selecting and hanging onto poor leaders, a mediocre work environment and, worse yet, bankruptcy. The results of this research put tremendous accountability and responsibility for business success into the hands of the work force like never before. This type of success cannot be experienced without absolute and uncompromising support from the top down, including leadership roles and the HR organization that holds responsibility for ensuring that all people systems are linked.

Without a doubt, HR's active and unconditional support of the learning effort is essential. This is only possible if the HR staff has a solid, respectful and trusting relationship with management, individual contributors and executive-level staff. Whoever is charged with the learning initiative (whether it's an individual or a team), he or she must have earned respect throughout the organization as someone who has a strong business acumen and a strategic focus as well as someone who can be counted on, who can lead, who can exhibit grace under pressure and who can masterfully build and maintain relationships, no matter the circumstances.

Management That Nobody Wants to Leave— That's a Good Thing

In this environment, managers know their stuff, and they know how to play to the strengths of those they lead. They focus on the strengths of employees and spend far less time on the problem areas. They hire smart and develop talent. They help employees connect the dots between their own behavior indicators (competencies) and individual goals, operational goals, business strategy, core values and company vision. This becomes routine as they become masterful in managing the linking of people systems and putting those systems into action. They also show an exceptional ability to reward, motivate and recognize those that achieve the mindset of learning the business. They don't just take in anyone who's breathing. They take appropriate action with non-performers. In this environment, a company does not experience loss of talent; people stay. Retention is a bottom-line strength. This is a good thing since the number one reason people quit jobs is poor relationships or bad experiences with their managers. You need great managers. A company retains talent when it has managers for whom people want to work and do business with day in and day out. Talent is your source of an engaged work force, a work force within which learning is the dominant mindset and focus.

Champions in Every Corner

In this environment, champions are identified and then let loose to create, perform, lead, succeed and celebrate efforts that increase the bottom line. Individuals who make learning the business their business make the unexpected happen. They also become a definite influence on those around them, creating an enticing and captivating energy that is quite contagious. Champions can be found in management, human resources, technology, functional organizations, etc. They exist in every corner of an organization. When learning is expected, champions rise up, and the environment encourages them to assume roles and handle responsibilities that tie their thoughts, words and actions to bottom-line measurements. They know how to position themselves to play to their strengths, and they work with management to make it so. They positively impact retention, profits, productivity, global competitiveness and customer satisfaction. They understand that this is a result of a full command of their behavior indicators (competencies) and determining competency-based goals. In turn, these goals are aligned with organization strategy and business measures. These people walk the talk and influence those around them to do the same. They are alignment savvy and cannot be persuaded to think, act or speak otherwise.

"Learning—It's Everybody's Business"— A Quick Assessment

Take a moment to review and then answer the questions in this quick assessment. It will give you a good idea of your current state of readiness for learning the business. When you begin to put the ideas in this chapter into action, you can then use this assessment to get a clear picture of your starting point.

Directions: Read each question and answer either YES or NO. When you decide what steps you are going to take, refer back to this assessment and make sure your efforts focus on the components to which you answered NO. Realize that working on any of the components affects the balance of the others. You need to ensure that working on one component does not duplicate any process, practice or policy that may exist in another component. It is best to build on what currently exists and refrain from any duplication of effort. This is why you need to have a full working knowledge of all components, even if you responded to any of them with a YES. It is a smart practice to periodically check for balance between all components and recalibrate as needed.

1. Do you have agreement among your key executives (those with the most influence, people systems knowledge and awareness, and relationship skills) that learning the business directly links individuals in the organization with measurable business outcomes such as customer satisfaction, retention (of both high performers and customers), productivity and profitability?

YES   NO

2. Is the concept of "Learning—It's Everybody's Business" evident in the vision, core values and business strategic plan?

YES   NO

3. Is the concept of "Learning—It's Everybody's Business" evident in operational plans and goals at the business unit and individual level?

YES   NO

4. Do company communications (intranet, Internet, employee news-letters, etc.) convey the message that learning is everybody's business?

YES   NO

5. Are all people systems (compensation, employee relations, organization development, staffing, training, etc.) linked with the behavioral indicators that are aligned with the vision and core values?

YES   NO

6. Do individual performance measurements align with the vision, core values and business strategy?

YES   NO

7. Are there processes/tools in place to track the direct link between individuals learning the business and business outcomes such as customer satisfaction, global competitiveness, retention (of both high performers and customers), productivity and profitability?

YES   NO

The recommendations that conclude this chapter will assume that you answered NO to each of the assessment questions. These recommendations will provide you with suggested steps to create, implement and measure a "Learning—It's Everybody's Business" initiative in the workplace.

Recommendations

For the purposes of this chapter, let's assume that there is satisfactory support for the initiative at the executive level and that you are the HR staff member identified to lead this initiative, and you have been given the go ahead to identify and select a team to lead the workforce in the Learning...It's Everybody's Business initiative. The value of a team is immeasurable for an initiative that has such a penetrating and personal impact on every individual in the organization. A team will help distribute the huge responsibility and task of creating momentum, excitement, enthusiasm, and staying power for this initiative. When peers lead peers there is also greater respect and willingness to learn and be open to a change on the part of individuals. The success of this initiative is highly dependent on individuals taking responsibility and ownership for their part in making it work. The shift to a mindset of self-responsibility and accountability is much more successful with this type of peer support and encouragement.

From start to finish, suppose a time frame of sixteen to twenty-four months for full implementation, complete people systems linking, having measurement systems in place to provide data that will identify what is going well, identifying obstacles that can then be addressed and demonstrating a direct link between the work force and business measures.

There are continuous benefits experienced at every juncture of this initiative. You will not have to wait sixteen to twenty-four months to show the results and to experience some definite positive changes, including a direct impact on the bottom line.

For you to be successful, it is important that you:

1. Establish yourself as a regular presenter on the agenda of executive staff meetings and management staff meetings throughout this entire initiative. Management needs to be constantly briefed, kept in the loop and given specific direction and follow-up expectations when it comes to communicating learning the business to the entire work force.

2. Identify and select the right team members for this initiative.

3. Plan and facilitate a high-energy and highly interactive team kickoff, which I refer to as a team-building/working session.

Prior to providing you with the recommended action steps for "Learning—It's Everybody's Business," I will offer some detailed suggestions regarding the executive and management meetings, team selection process and team-building/working sessions for you to consider

Briefing Sessions with the Executive Staff

Your first order of business is to establish a practice of holding briefing sessions with your executive level of support. This includes your HR vice-president and your executive-level staff members (which, depending on the structure of your organization, includes your CEO). Make it clear that this is a business practice and that you will adhere to it. Convey that you consider this briefing opportunity good for the business.

The purpose of the briefing sessions is to convey your intentions, specific plans and progress to the executive staff. It is critical that each clearly understands that the high-level goals of this initiative are to align all efforts with the business vision, core values, strategy and operations goals and to link all people systems, demonstrating a direct relationship between people and business outcomes. It is important for you to be prepared with a great deal of data during these briefing sessions so that you present facts that can become the basis for any decisions that must be made to maintain forward momentum.

It is recommended that after the initial meeting you attend an executive staff meeting once a quarter in the first year of the initiative and every other quarter the second year. Your job will be to review progress, answer any questions and discuss any adjustments that may surface. Your job is to help everyone clearly see that learning the business benefits them, the work force and the bottom line.

Your initial executive staff briefing will include:

1. Review "Learning—It's Everybody's Business" high-level goals and action steps.

2. Identify team members, select them and facilitate a team-building/working session to kick off the initiative.

3. Review the time commitment you need from each of the team members. Express that you need his full support during this time so that each knows that he has support during the time away from his own assigned responsibilities.

4. Ask each executive to identify the key employees that he knows will be contributors to this team. They may need a couple of days to respond. They may choose to filter this down through their managers, especially those on the front line, to identify individual contributors who are high-potential performers.

   a. It's important that you control this identification process by giving each executive a five-business-day deadline to talk with her management staff, identify potential team members and get back to you with individuals' names and contact information. It is also important that you provide a paragraph that explains why each has been identified and what being a team member is all about. This is really important, because the message can get mixed up and poorly communicated. Potential team members need to receive a consistent and seamless message.

Note: Often, executives delegate this task to one or each of their front-line managers. In this case, you should follow up with that person.

    b. Once you receive recommendations, review for balance among functional business units and support units. Be sure there is a balance of members across business units.

Briefing Sessions with Front-line Management

It is imperative that your front-line managers be fully educated and aware of the action plans, how the plans will affect their business unit operations, expected changes and the impact on current policy and practices related to people systems. You will need to spend much of your time walking managers through changes to policy and practices, because they are going to need to learn new ways of doing things. (Example: Managers may need to learn a new way to administer the performance-management process.)

Plan to attend each business unit staff meeting and request forty-five minutes on the agenda. These briefings can begin to take place during your identification and selection process of team members. The executive staff will involve front-line management in the team-member-recommendation process, so it is the right time to meet with them. In fact, as soon as you get the green light in the executive-level staff meeting, coordinate the briefing sessions with front-line management.

Plan to brief front-line management four to six times in the first year and four times in the second year of the initiative. Follow the agenda recommendation below for each of your meetings.

Recommended Front-line Management Briefing Session Agenda

1. Spend twenty minutes explaining the overall initiative, including the "why," the "what" and the "how." Company benefits and, of course, what's in it for them and their employees should be explained as well.

2. Spend ten minutes stressing the top-down, executive-level support and direct impact on business outcomes.

3. Spend ten minutes reviewing a general sixteen to twenty-four-month project timeline with them.

4. Spend the final five minutes on Q & A.

Team Leader Identification

Rather than attempt to lead solo, it is best to identify a team to lead the initiative with you. It is best to form a team so the responsibilities of leading can be shared. It is very important that an individual from the human resources organization (you) be identified as a leader since HR has a direct responsibility for people system policy, practice and linking. Once leaders are identified, a team consisting of management, HR and individual contributors who will carry out the creation, implementation and measurement of a learning-the-business initiative needs to be selected.

Team Member Selection

Team composition as just described is the ideal situation. Having genuine, top-down support at the executive level is your signal to forge ahead. Careful identification and selection of the team from the HR organization, a pool of high-performing individual contributors and managers representing functional and support organizations are so important. You need to do this right from the start. Mistakes in the identification of the team members can create constant interference and irritation and radically hinder the progress. This can become a negative force within the team and exhaust members. Further, this weakens the message to the work force overall and limits your success at embedding the idea of learning the business into the work environment.

Team Size

You need to determine the number of people it will take to represent the company in a balanced manner and to include a good mix of management, support functions (such as HR) and individual contributors who are high performers. As a reference, I have worked with different ratios, such as 1:25, 1:50 and 1:100. Just be sure to use sound judgment and understand that a good mix is most important.

Team-building/Working Sessions—Kickoff

Once your team has been identified and selected, you and your co-leaders need to organize and facilitate what I call a team-building/working session. This session is a combination of team building (keynote statements from top management, icebreakers, developmental exercises, sharing expectations, etc.) and working sessions. During the working session portion, team members are educated and oriented to the concept of "Learning—It's Everybody's Business." During this portion of the session, participants receive a great deal of information. They are divided into breakout groups (four or five people), and they participate in planning detailed action steps for the major strategies: strategy management, communication and marketing, tools and people systems linking. They also spend time identifying obstacles to the major strategies and solutions to those obstacles.

Once this is accomplished, they reconvene to their breakout groups and begin to develop detailed action plans and business outcome measurements for each strategy that will help achieve an environment in which learning is everybody's business. This activity takes time and needs to be continued beyond the working session. As a result, teams are formed within the overall team, and each one focuses on a particular strategy, its action plans and its planned business outcomes. Prior to the conclusion of the working session, the team agrees on its ground rules, how each major strategy team will operate, who will lead each strategy team and the meeting schedule for the team as a whole.

The team-building/working session is critical to the team members building strong and enduring relationships with each other and to their developing loyalty and commitment to the learning-the-business initiative. When planning this working session, you need to be sure that it is in a location where participants cannot be disturbed and can focus completely on the task at hand. Ideally, this working session requires two full successive days of team building and planning. You can organize this time differently if you choose, but be careful. You can plan one full day and two half-days or four half-days or some other combination. Be sure that the way you schedule the sessions preserves the momentum of the team building. The momentum needs to be a priority, and the team members must walk away energized and ready to dedicate their time and focus to achieving the planned strategies. Breaking the session into smaller increments can throw off this important element of focus, energy and motivation among the team members. Team members are usually very supportive and able to adjust their schedules for the two-day commitment. You may get resistance from those not involved in the team who feel that is too much time for someone to be away from his job tasks. Usually, these individuals are managers. It's not always the case, but often, the most resistant managers are also the mediocre managers, not the great ones! Lean on your VP and the executive staff to continually send a strong message of support for this initiative.

Four Strategy Teams for "Learning— It's Everybody's Business"

It is recommended that the "Learning—It's Everybody's Business" team be developed around four major strategy teams—*strategy management, people systems linking, tools, marketing and communication.* These teams will focus on specific areas of delivery for the initiative. Based on your organization's makeup, you may see a need for more strategy teams. That's for you and the team to determine.

Organizing into the four strategy teams will ensure that the "Learning—It's Everybody's Business" team becomes part of decisions and is able to influence company policies, practices, communications and all people systems. This prevents any possibility of the team and the initiative becoming isolated from the business strategy and falling by the wayside.

"Learning—It's Everybody's Business" Strategy Teams and Recommended Action Steps

I. Strategy Management Team

This team guides learning-the-business efforts to ensure a direct link with business outcomes. This team works tirelessly to coordinate the identification of behavior indicators (competencies) and the communication of these behavior indicators to the work force as well as guide the process of linking people systems with these behavior indicators. This team is critical to ensuring that behavior indicators are aligned with business vision, core values, strategy and business goals. This team figures out how to measure business outcomes as the results of a work environment in which learning is everybody's business.

Examples of Strategy Management Team Action Steps

1. Coordinate and facilitate focus groups across the organization in order to gather baseline data for the initiative. (Consider using the twelve questions that stem from the research found in *First, Break All The Rules*. I referenced this book and research earlier in the chapter.)

2. Coordinate a process of identifying behavior indicators (competencies) across the organization. Provide a high-level process for educating the work force on the behavior indicators, showing how these behaviors are aligned with the vision, core values, strategy, operational goals and all people-linking systems. This is an action step that needs to be taken in conjunction with the people systems linking team.

3. Evaluate current tools and resources (performance-management process, monthly communications, training courses/methods, etc.) within the company and determine which are aligned with company vision, core values, strategy and operational goals. This is an action step that needs to be completed along with the people systems linking team, which will review results from the perspective of alignment.

4. Establish baseline business results measurements—retention, customer satisfaction, productivity and profit. Set a schedule for the ongoing gathering of data so that you have numbers to show. (Consider using the twelve questions that stem from the research found in *First, Break All The Rules*.) Further, this data will aid you in recommending any adjustments to the action steps of the initiative. Develop a method for having a continual presence at executive staff and front-line management meetings for the purpose of reporting status. Establish a partnership with front-line managers to make sure they do what they need to do in support of the initiatives and that they receive as much assistance and guidance possible throughout the entire process. Influence executive staff to include a specific strategy about "Learning—It's Everybody's Business" in the annual and long-term strategic-planning documents.

5. Develop a checks-and-balances system within the team to be sure that each strategy team's action plan is in alignment, its efforts are not being duplicated and it is accomplishing what it set out to do.

6. Choose and implement a means of tracking the entire project. Identify at least two individuals within this strategy team to manage this project tool.

7. Develop a high-level communication series (if it does not exist) to teach the business to the work force. Give it the information to learn the business. Include definitions and explanations of business, finance, strategy, marketing, etc. Organize the communication in a way that the people systems linking team can incorporate materials into any training initiatives that it is planning. Include a model for alignment so that it is clear how the work force directly impacts the bottom line through various business measures.

8. Create a recognition program for the work force that provides incentives to learn the business, and reward it when it does so. The recognition parameters need to be associated with the business measures of retention, customer satisfaction, productivity and profit.

II. People Systems Linking Team

This team keeps everyone informed and involved in understanding the team strategies and how they benefit the company and the individual. This team works closely with each of the other teams, primarily with the HR organization, to execute the linking of people systems. Ensure that changes in policies and practices as a result of people systems linking are well communicated to each and every employee. This team also works closely with the training entities within the organization to be sure that the entire work force is constantly educated in all aspects of learning the business. It is logical to assign team members that are from the HR organization to this team.

Examples of People Systems Linking Team Action Steps

1. Review each HR function's system (training, compensation/performance management, staffing, communications) and gain a full and complete understanding of policy, practice, resources and tools. Based on this review, lay out a detailed plan for linking each people system with the identified behavior indicators. The goal is to be sure that the same criteria used to staff the organization are also used to manage the performance of the organization and the training of the organization. Example: If the

behavior indicators/competencies for hiring a manager are business acumen, communication, relationship skills, cost consciousness, problem solving, vision, project planning and team leading, then the performance criteria and training plan need to be based on the same behavior indicators.

2. Make sure there is a plan to fully and completely communicate the behavior indicators/competencies to all of the work force and ensure that it understands its direct link to business outcomes.

- ♦ This needs to be done in a format by which each person fully understands the competencies and how each relates to his or her job tasks, the operational goals, the business strategy, the core values and company vision. This is an education in the "how."

- ♦ Further, the work force must be educated in each of the people systems; self-management of these systems is critical to learning the business. Example: A person must know what behavior indicators relate to her position and then understand how to identify and write training goals related to her role. Further, she must understand how these individual goals relate to the bigger picture and business measures of retention, customer satisfaction, productivity and profit.

- ♦ In conjunction with the strategy management team, the people systems linking team designs a training series that will clearly communicate the entire scope of "Learning—It's Everybody's Business." Every detail emphasizing what's in it for them must be communicated. This is an ongoing process.

III. Tools/Processes Team

This team enhances and develops tools (Web-based and otherwise) that support learning the business initiatives. It is a key responsibility of this team to build on currently existing tools and processes and avoid duplicating any efforts. This team is also charged with implementing solutions that take advantage of the latest and greatest technology. This team also helps each of the other teams implement its action plans using the best resources and technology possible.

Examples of Tool/Processes Team Action Steps

1. Review existing tools/process and determine how to enhance rather than duplicate. Tools/processes for people systems include performance management, training management, rewards/incentives and goal setting.

2. Create a Web site for "Learning—It's Everybody's Business" components and make sure that all aspects of learning are linked to this site. Make sure that all people systems are included on this site.

3. Personalize the Web site for each employee so that each can manage, track and adjust his own learning goals. It is imperative that each employee assumes ownership and responsibility for his success in learning the business.

4. Develop training guides for any tools that are used by the work force. Ensure that there is a rollout and training plan for each of the tools.

5. Review current technology and be sure that each of the tools is developed with the latest and greatest that the company can support. This will help avoid problems when the tools are turned on.

IV. Marketing/Communication Team

This team communicates and markets learning initiatives to the work force. This team makes sure that at every turn the work force sees evidence of "Learning—It's Everybody's Business." Whether in conference rooms, hallways, the cafeteria, the break room, etc., the work force has some reference that points to the initiative, ongoing progress checks, testimonials, events, new tools or resources, contests and companywide recognition.

Examples of Marketing/Communication Team Action Steps

1. Review current marketing and communication formats.

2. Market "Learning—It's Everybody's Business" in company communications, on the learning Web site, on the intranet and on the Internet. Market it in any publication format that currently exists.

3. Market the high-level purpose of this initiative. Through various methods, bombard the work force with company vision, core val-

ues, business strategy and operational goals. Show the direct tie to the business measures of learning the business.

4. Market the "Learning—It's Everybody's Business" teams so that the work force becomes aware and knowledgeable of the individuals involved in the effort and the action steps that are being implemented.

5. Coordinate and hold information sessions and Q & A sessions to encourage constant talk and communication about the initiative.

6. Use various advertising methods to recognize progress and individuals throughout the entire initiative.

Conclusion

The recommended project steps involved in creating a "Learning—It's Everybody's Business" mindset are quite involved and require your constant attention and total commitment. This chapter cannot possibly drill down to that level of detail. It will be up to you to glean everything you can from this chapter and build a solid platform from which you can launch your own customized "Learning—It's Everybody's Business" initiative. One thing I know for sure is that you can support everything you do with numbers that now directly link people systems to business results. I've done it with success, and I have worked with individuals just like you to help work forces adopt the mindset that learning is everybody's business. I know it can be done.

Therese M. Malm, MA

 Therese Malm is dedicated to transforming today's challenges into tomorrow's successes for individuals as well as organizations. For over fifteen years, Therese has concentrated her efforts on the delivery of products and services focused on what will work short and long term (solution focused), rather than on what won't work (problem focused). This is the distinction that makes the difference for her company. Therese received her BS from the University of Wisconsin—Madison and her MA-Human Resources from Truman State University. Therese consults in the areas of: alignment of the workforce with business strategy, teambuilding working sessions, leadership development, employee development, performance management and development, learning organization development, and creating synergy between people strategies and business goals. Therese also offers a unique business solution related to management of your human resources. TM Consulting Group will partner with you to handle all of your Employee Relations matters, Compensation, Performance Management, Training, and Staffing. This partnership will save you much of your valuable time while building the trust and confidence of your employees in the fair and management of your HR practices and policies. The versatility of TM Consulting Group is evident in the breadth of offerings available.

TM Consulting Group: Therese M. Malm, MA
Transforming Today's Challenges into Tomorrow's Successes
Business Phone: 847-571-7909 * FAX: 847-695-4977
Email: tmconsultinggroup@msn.com
194 Gregory M. Sears Drive
Gilberts, IL 60136

Chapter Seven

Hey, HR—Wake Up And Get To The Table!

Jim Tait

Are you an HR professional who feels left out of the "value chain"? Do you find yourself uninvited to critical strategic planning sessions in your business? Are other functional leaders within the organization supporting you verbally but undermining HR systems and processes through their actions or the actions of their teams? If so, then in all likelihood you are an HR leader who is still asleep. Seven years ago, American HR and business leaders received a wake-up call that went unanswered and turned the theory of succession into a stark reality. U.S. Commerce Secretary Ron Brown and twelve CEOs of multi-industry organizations were traveling on an airplane that crashed into a Croatian mountainside. In a moment, twelve companies lost the luxury of time to plan ahead.

Some of those twelve organizations may have moved into their succession plans smoothly, while others surely moved into an emergency state of management and found themselves making many difficult and, in some cases, wrong, decisions.

The stark and factual realization precipitated by that disaster was both extreme and sobering. Fortunately, most changes in leadership are not initiated by catastrophe or the untimely death of a leader but instead are due to the need of a change in relationship between the leader and the organization he or she is leading. Leaders are not invincible or perpetual, either as individuals or in the roles they occupy.

In the early morning hours of September 11, 2001, the world watched in horror as commercial jetliners crashed into the World Trade Center twin towers, the Pentagon and a field in Pennsylvania. The loss of civilian life and the destruction of corporate property were beyond what we could have imagined and yet were clearly a reality. The five-year-long wake-up call for many American HR and business leaders had gone unanswered. Should you desire to remain asleep and/or simply remain an HR professional who can't get to the decision-making table, then skip ahead to the next chapter. If not, read on.

Even before the towers collapsed and anyone had a chance to grieve, many organizations had to face the fact that they had lost key employees who were on the planes or in the buildings. The list of organizations that were most severely affected included Akamai, BEA Systems, Cantor Fitzgerald, Cisco Systems, 3Com, the Fire Department of New York, Oracle, Raytheon and Sun Microsystems.

Suddenly these companies, their employees, customers and suppliers faced a very different and uncertain future. They not only had to manage the reality that key leadership, knowledge and intellectual property were gone but they also had to confront the significant vacancies in their management structure. They immediately had to identify the roles, relationships and skill sets that were required just to stay afloat.

There's no way to plan for a catastrophe of the horrific significance of the September 11th attacks or the airplane crash into the Croatian mountainside. However, there are specific steps you can take to prepare for unexpected events. Not surprisingly, many organizations are taking a close look at what's required to keep a business running if key executives suddenly leave—not only because of catastrophes but because of other opportunities, burnout, changes in the business or perhaps something a little more racy, like a jail term imposed because of insider trading or accounting fraud.

Succession planning is not simple, but if done right, it can clearly define you as a business person who just happens to manage an HR function. Mapping the organization of the future involves more than developing a proposed organizational chart outlining the corporate structure. Any old-school personnel manager can handle that. It's imperative for a contemporary HR leader to know which employees have the skills, competencies and organizational credibility required to effectively assume positions with greater responsibility, what talents will be required in the future and how best to either develop employees for leadership positions or recruit from the outside. Succession planning may include the use of a wide range of tools, from a spreadsheet or simple database to sophisticated software for tracking previous performance, competencies and 360-degree feedback data.

Best-practice organizations use succession planning to prepare for the future needs of the company. However, they also rely on such plans to further develop the strong leadership that's required on a day-to-day basis. A well-managed succession plan will help an organization keep pace with changes in the company, industry and the overall economy. It will help the enterprise focus on the performance of its human capital.

Despite the obvious need for a succession plan, companies and their HR leaders (a term that, for the most part, is overused and, in some cases, oxymoronic) still don't answer the wake-up call. Duhh! According to survey data, forty-five percent of boards at companies with sales of more than $500 million have no meaningful process for developing potential leaders. And, astonishingly, twenty-four percent of Fortune 500 companies don't consider succession planning a top priority. Where is that elusive HR leadership? Not at the table, apparently.

What does it take to develop a succession plan that's suited to an organization's specific needs? How should an enterprise structure a plan? And what role should human resources play in the process? An effective succession plan requires a careful examination of business strategy. Therefore, you as an HR professional need to get to the business information that will allow you to influence leadership to make the human resource decisions that will add value and drive viability.

In decades past, developing and promoting talent was a fairly simple proposition. The leadership of a company decided who would be slotted into a senior management position—a decision usually based on hunches, instincts and intuition. If the CEO or president resigned or retired, the number two person almost always assumed the top post. In most instances, the person next in line knew well ahead of time that the company was grooming him or her for the job. Grooming is for pets. Succession planning and management resourcing are for companies and HR professionals that want to win.

In today's fast-changing, global, business environment, however, deciding who the future leaders will be without multilevel, multifunctional and, in many cases, multilingual input and dialogue is no longer effective. Although senior-level positions remain a key to an organization's success, there needs to be the realization that the entire management structure determines how a company acts and reacts to industry conditions and global events. It is your job to hammer that point home. As the events of September 11th indicated, a company's fortunes can change in a heartbeat. Bond-trading firm Cantor Fitzgerald lost 700 of its 1,000 World Trade Center workers, including many top executives. At the Fire Department of New York, 343 employees died, including some of its highest-ranking administrators and executives. Would it be fair to say that the HR functions of these two organizations were relied upon by operational leadership to help them rebuild? Probably so—but what a caustic event to bring about that reliance!

Although the sudden loss of a key executive is always a possibility, a company should be focused on developing talent over the long term. There is a tremendous amount of expertise within most companies, and it's impossible to replace it overnight.

A well-designed succession-planning system allows HR and senior management to adapt more quickly to rapidly changing business conditions, including new competitors, customers and economies. Instead of senior leadership spending a great deal of time interviewing many candidates, it's possible to immediately zero in on the best candidate based on the needs of business, functional area and employees. Then, when a position opens up, it's clear who is prepared to fill it internally or whether the company should look outside for additional talent.

There is no standard template for creating a succession-planning system. It's a process that requires ongoing review and scrutiny as well as leadership from HR and ownership by the CEO and other leaders. It's important to understand what's required to run the company in the future rather than making decisions based on immediate needs. Come on—admit it. If a senior executive left your company, wouldn't it be nice if the CEO came immediately to you and wanted to spend a couple of hours reviewing the succession plan? Who are the high potentials? Who are the promotables? Who is ready now? Who will be ready in one or two years? Who backfills that person? Can we move this one into a cross-functioned assignment? Would it not be impressive to have that information immediately available? Think of the true impact you could have on the organization by driving the management of the human capital. Don't just think about; do it.

When it's done right, succession planning is an investment in both the company and the employees of the organization. The entire organization can benefit by creating career paths and developing criteria to fill various positions. Then, whether a change is required because of normal business conditions or death, disaster or defection, an organization is ready to act quickly, decisively and effectively. Only then can a company know it is able to conduct business as usual, even in the most unusual of times.

In recent years, succession planning has evolved in both scope and complexity.

Yet many organizations and HR people who may have started to awaken go back to sleep when it comes to implementing an effective succession plan. They engage in replacement planning. They ask managers to fill out forms and suggest who should be promoted but then don't bother to review regularly or, in many cases, even use the process they have, thus alienating workers, peers and their leadership further. There's nothing like stepping away from the table after having been invited.

Identifying top talent is usually the easy part. It's providing people with the skill sets and experience necessary to become effective and lasting leaders that presents a challenge. In order to develop future leaders, it's essential to inform the high-potential employees that they are in an acceleration pool and develop them cross-functionally within an organization to gain expertise and experience. The fact that they're considered for future leadership can prove to be a motivator and significant retention tool.

And while software and systems are important elements in managing succession planning, they cannot fix underlying processes that are broken. Ultimately, succession planning/management is a people-oriented process, from top to bottom. It's up to senior executives to take ownership, HR to analyze and lead, and line managers to evaluate and measure. Only then can an organization avoid placing employees into positions before they're ready and making a tenuous time worse.

What is involved in succession planning? Succession planning is a part of the process of preparing the organization for the future of your company. It is suggested that virtually every key position and key person in your organization is a candidate for a succession plan. An important point to make is that it is virtually impossible to successfully promote someone unless there is a trained person to take over the position being vacated. To effectively implement a succession plan, you need to include and consider a number of the following elements and answer the following questions:

1. What is the long-term business direction of your company? Do you have an effective strategic business plan guiding this course and direction? If so, do you know what it is? Can you communicate it to others?

2. What are the key areas that require continuity and development of the people resources within your company? Look at research and development, sales and marketing, manufacturing, information systems, finance, procurement, etc.

3. Who are the key people who need to be developed for the future?

4. How does the concept of succession planning fit into your business strategies? Are you concentrating your efforts in the areas where the returns for the business will be highest?

5. What are the career paths your most talented people should be following? Is each path customized with action plans, timing and accountability to fit the needs and capabilities of the people and the business? The point here is to be sure you do not do this by utilizing too much structure and process. A plan that is not dynamic, that does not include the consideration of the individuals involved, is not as effective as one that is tailored to the mutual needs and capabilities of the employee and the company.

6. Should you wait for openings to appear before promoting someone, or should you make opportunities for each individual as they grow and mature, so that you can keep them challenged and stimulated and not lose them to other, possibly faster-moving, companies? If you would like to remain and prosper in HR, your plan should be proactive—with people moving into different areas for experience and training before they are needed in critical times—rather than reactive—waiting for openings to occur, then scurrying around to find an appropriate candidate at the last second.

What strategies should you be considering for your succession-planning process? First, realize that one size doesn't fit all. There are different approaches that need to be used, depending on the situation in each function of a company. In some cases, a company may have to move applications engineers along quickly in order to expose them to a broad range of customer issues and possibly to fill vacancies in research and development. In others, a deeper involvement in selected departments or disciplines may be required. Some of this will depend on the culture and products of the company. And in other cases, decisions will depend on the individual's capabilities and competencies as well as the future structure and operations of the company. For example, you may be currently exercising due diligence on a foreign entity. You may have a high-potential operations leader who is targeted for greater responsibility after the acquisition. Should you expose this employee to an assignment in purchasing, in light of the fact that you buy a large percentage of your raw material from companies in the country that is home to the company you wish to acquire? In virtually all situations, your ability to influence, educate and promote will depend not only on the capabilities and strengths of the people who currently occupy the key positions but where they will be going in the future. You now have the responsibility for influencing and brokering decisions that will have the potential to make or break. How could you not be excited by the opportunity here? You are now aligning broad organizational needs with critical employee needs, potentially saving thousands of dollars in recruiting and relocation costs and improving productivity through reduced learning curves. Employee satisfaction is up, and voluntary turnover is down. How could you possibly be asleep?

It may not be vital to have a succession plan for every position in the company, but certainly there are some key areas of responsibility that must be considered. These will vary by company and industry, but as a part of your process, one important strategic issue should be the need for succession for certain defined, key positions. This issue should be revisited at least twice a year and more often if circumstances dictate. You have to make this happen.

While it may be redundant, assume a Catbert, the Evil HR Director type, is still with us, doubting the value of the process, and still needs to have a few of the many advantages of succession planning laid out.

- An evolving supply of well-trained, cross-functional, deeply experienced, motivated employees who are able to step into key positions as business conditions demand.
- A bank of company-knowledgeable candidates who are being further integrated into the organization with individual career goals and paths established for them.

- A value-based movement of these high-potential employees through various departments with the goal of further educating them into the culture and processes of the company.

- Alignment of the future needs of the business with the availability of appropriate human resources within the company.

- Relevant and meaningful goals for key personnel, which will help keep them focused and assure the continuing supply of capable successors for the critically defined positions included in the succession plan.

- Dynamic and defined career paths, which will recruit and retain the best possible candidates and employees.

- The continuous input of out-of-the-box ideas from high-potential people in new areas, which will improve the internal business processes and systems of the company as well as the products and services of the company in the marketplace.

Recognize that businesses do not have to follow the same path in the overall succession plan situation or even for each individual. Each action should be analyzed and leveraged in terms of the company's needs and the individual's needs. In addition, there should be mutually agreed upon timeframes allowing for the development of the successors. They should not be expected to perform the jobs/responsibilities overnight. Also, the successor and potential backups should be designated and the plan communicated early in the process to prevent frustration and disillusionment. High performers need to know they are being developed for positions with more scope and complexity and they will benefit from knowing the proposed timeline.

There are no downsides to developing, deploying and standardizing a succession planning process; however, there are some things you need to avoid:

1. Not having a formal written and communicated developmental action plan for each key person or position.
2. Having a rigid plan that is NOT synergistically tailored to the developmental needs and abilities of the employees and departments involved.

3. Allowing too much time to pass before real movement/promotion that could result in the high-potential employees leaving due to apparent broken promises.

4. Selection of poor performers or manage-out candidates for inclusion in the succession plan. The credibility and quality of the individual selected is critical to the overall success of the process.

How does succession planning fit into your company's overall strategic planning process? As in the deployment and utilization of any strategic resource, the development of your key people must be considered as you plan for the future of your company. It is certainly worth considerable time and effort to thoroughly discuss as a strategic issue the company's needs and current capabilities. If you do not have a formal procedure for succession planning, you may want to create an objective that mandates the development and installation of a succession-planning process that fits the needs and preferences of your specific company. What do you need to do to get the best from your people, to position and educate them so that they may best contribute to the company's (and their own) long-term success and to assure a flow of competent, well-educated and experienced people for your future?

How long should succession planning take? Realistically, succession planning is never finished. On a regular basis, each company must look at its needs and resources to determine where it should have successors in place or in the process of learning the requisite disciplines. Each company needs to determine how long a candidate should be involved in or exposed to the training needed. Each individual should have a concisely determined path toward the goal set for him or her. That path may be changed as needed and as events determine, so monitoring and updating is a critical aspect of every succession plan.

Over what time period should you plan? To be realistic, succession must be planned years in advance of expected needs. To properly train a successor, the company needs sufficient time to expose the people to the full spectrum of opportunities within the organization as well as any desired or required outside education/experience. For example, if someone is expected to be a general manager, the number of departments, the types and ranges of technologies and processes, and the level of knowledge about the company procedures and policies, markets and customers, suppliers, employees, contractors, etc., will determine the time and depth of involvement. Additional factors such as past experience, current knowledge and organizational credibility that the individual brings to the process will also affect the succession time frame.

Let's get you started with some basic process tools. This should work for any company, big or small.

We'll start with your leadership team, the direct reports of your boss. This tool is called the Leadership Assessment Summary.

LEADERSHIP ASSESSMENT SUMMARY
DIRECT REPORTS

Sit down with your leader and chart the leadership of these individuals. When discussing how far along the right hand side of the axis an individual's behaviors are, think about the values of the organization. Does he or she treat others with dignity and respect, demonstrate strategic thinking capabilities and display a bias for action? Is he/she results-oriented? Does he/she demonstrate organizational courage, manage by facts and delegate effectively? How far a person is placed up the Results side of the axis should be defined relatively easily. Does he make his numbers? Do not be surprised to find individuals who may have tremendous results with below-standard behavior. They should not be defined as high-potential employees until the behaviors change. And they need to be informed of this. Each organization will need to define for itself the

140

term "potential" as it applies to an individual. A starting point, or general rule of thumb, for you may be the following:

High Potential (Ten Percent of Organization)	An individual who is capable of making two vertical career moves within a five-year time frame. The end result would be a position with significantly more scope and complexity, with far greater responsibility for dollars, people, capital resources, decisions, etc. This person consistently exceeds all expectations and outperforms all metrics.
Promotable (Twenty Percent of Organization)	An individual who is capable of making one vertical career move within a five-year time frame. The end result would be a position with more scope and complexity and greater responsibility for dollars, people, capital resources, decisions, etc. This person occasionally exceeds and never misses high expectations.
Experienced Professional (Sixty Percent of Organization)	A strong individual contributor or manager that is highly competent, respected and continues to meet raised expectations.
Manage Out (Ten Percent of Organization)	This individual needs to be removed from the position and/or the organization. An upgrade in talent should be moved in from the succession plan or from outside the company. This person is either not meeting or will not in the future meet raised expectations.
Too New	This person has typically been with the organization or in a new role for fewer than six months.

This tool should be cascaded as deeply into the organization as practical. At a minimum, it should include all salaried employees.

Once you have secured your leadership's buy-in, move by functional leader throughout the company.

The next tool we need to look at is the High Potential Summary. A similar document should be utilized for the promotable population. These are self-explanatory and should be utilized for and during senior leadership discussions around "next steps" for succession candidates.

NAME TITLE LOCATION	SALARY	CODES	HIGHEST ATTAINABLE POSITION	AVAILABILITY ISSUES
Mary	$100,000	P	Plant Manager	Ready in 1-2 years
Joe	$85,000	X	Manager	Ready in 5 years
Ed	$92,000	F	Plant Manager	Ready in 3 years

CODES:
W=Female, M=Minority, F=Cross Functional Potential, X=Cross Business Potential, P=Female/Minority

The succession plan document is clearly a tool that needs to be informally reviewed and managed on a regular basis. You and the owners of the plan (functional leaders, CEO types) should review it at least twice a year.

POSITION	INCUMBENT	NOW	1-2 YEARS	3-5 YEARS
GM	Mr. Big	Charlie	Mary / Ed	Bill

CODES:
W=Female, M=Minority (non-white, US Citizen), I=International (non US Citizen)

Let's review five key succession planning factors:

1. Identify key leadership criteria: It's essential that an organization know what skills and competencies it needs in order to succeed. No one group, including HR, can identify all these traits. As a result, successful organizations usually rely on broad leadership and employee input to better understand core competencies and personnel requirements.

2. Find future leaders and motivate them: An enterprise must have a system in place for finding high-potential and promotable employees and ensuring that they're ready for key positions. This can involve any of several informal discussions, including 360-degree feedback, standard reviews and informal discussions. Understanding employees' talents, aptitudes and interests—and then providing developmental and business-valuable assignments—creates a much higher likelihood of success than the sole utilization of a merit-based compensation system.

3. Create a sense of responsibility within the organization. Although HR can serve as a catalyst for effective succession planning, most successful organizations rely on senior leadership to review and oversee the progress of employees. Then, as employees develop, recorded and visible history of his or her progress exists, with review from various levels within the company.

4. Align succession planning with the corporate culture. Despite an emphasis on past performance, it is essential to retain a focus on core values. Effective succession planning requires an organization to stress these values, whether it's a desire to demonstrate leadership or achieve business results, and weight them as evenly as possible in the overall selection process.

5. Measure results and reinforce desired behavior: The only way to know whether a succession plan is effective is to put systems in place to track results and have the owners and HR review the overall effectiveness of the program. Then the organization must develop systems such as reward-based compensation, training and appropriate developmental assignments to motivate workers and push them along desired development paths.

Succession is about maintaining the continuity of an organization and its value. It is more than the raw transfer of intellectual property, power and the associated fortunes of promotion. It is about survival.

The value of succession planning is evident to the entrepreneurial founder of a small family company who must pass the reins of leadership to a son or daughter where the next generation's inheritance is on the line. However, leaders of companies face additional issues, even when potential successors are ready to step up to the CEO position. From the smallest mom-and-pop business to the largest billion-dollar megalith, the reality remains the same. The right decision increases the likelihood that the company will survive and prosper—a major concern, particularly in today's era of mergers and acquisitions, when organizations that falter cease to exist.

A healthy succession-planning process is central to a company's ability to sustain itself and survive. The process promotes the articulation of an organization's essential leadership qualities, stimulates discussion about the organization's leaders and provides disciplined actions that nurture successors. By following these processes, the leadership of a company is in the best position to identify and develop the most capable future leaders of the company.

By ignoring succession planning, an organization places itself at risk. And the risks are substantial: relying on untested leaders to guide an organization through uncertain times and placing the company's future in the hands of an individual who knows little of the company's values and ideals. Perhaps the greatest risk is surrendering control of the company's future leadership to the unknown. Most successful CEOs and the HR leaders who support them did not become successful by relying on chance to determine their fortunes. Why would you? You wouldn't, can't and won't.

Utilizing this process, you as an HR professional will drive and enhance value within the company. You will do this because you will be developing high-potential research and development engineers, procurement and finance professionals. You will do this because you are in regular dialogue with their functional leadership as well as the peer group of all the other functional leaders. You should have, and will maintain, the most highly integrated knowledge of each and every function within your company. The leadership team and your boss will come to rely on you as a true business partner. To really add value, you should be fully engaged and at the table when business-critical decisions are being made. So wake up and get to the table.

Jim Tait

James B. Tait (Jim) is Chairman and CEO of The Transition Team, Knoxville, as well as a Corporate Director and responsible for national and international client development. He is also Chairman of the Alliance of Tennessee Employers. Tait has 18 years of professional human resources experience with large multi-national corporations, including Union Carbide and Allied Signal. Prior to joining The Transition Team in 2000, he held the title of global vice president of human resources for Breed Technologies, a $1.5 billion automotive parts supplier. He has extensive experience in domestic and international labor and employee relations; strategic organizational design and development; executive staffing and coaching; divestitures, acquisitions, and management development. Jim and his partner, Les Lunceford, have just recently published their first book, From Pink Slip Blues to Successfully Starting Your New Job, and are working simultaneously on their second and third books, which are centered on leadership and Tennessee employment and labor laws respectively. Tait, his wife, Deann, and their five children have lived in Knoxville since 1994. A 1986 graduate of Syracuse University, where he received a bachelor's degree in human resources management, Tait was the recipient of a SU football scholarship.

James B. Tait
Chairman, The Alliance of Tennessee Employers, Inc. &
Chairman and CEO, The Transition Team - Knoxville
9111 Cross Park Drive, Suite A-250
Knoxville, TN 37923
865.694.3848
www.transitionteam.com

Chapter Eight

The Challenge Of Change

George Ritcheske

The challenge of change within an organization is difficult for leaders and employees alike. Leaders must embrace the new vision and find the courage to move in that new direction, not knowing all the steps to take and uncertain that the changes will eventually create a better organization. Employees must comprehend the vision and decipher how it will affect them; they need to be willing to proceed, based on trust in the leadership, into an unclear future. Yet the most difficult challenge when facing change belongs to the human resource group. Leaders expect them to be a source of advice and guidance during the transition. Meanwhile, HR professionals must continue to manage employee legal issues in ways that minimize risk for the organization while also ensuring compliance with local, state and federal employee laws. Employees depend on HR for accurate, timely information and the fair and efficient administration of compensation and benefits plans. Finally, HR also needs to lead the redesign of programs, processes and infrastructure so the transformed organization can operate effectively. This three-dimensional task—guidance, administration and redesign—can be daunting to the most seasoned HR professional and downright scary to those with less experience. However, all HR professionals can successfully meet the challenge by embracing the five guiding principles of navigating change:

1. **Paint the possibilities.**
2. **Increase the involvement.**
3. **Lead the learning.**
4. **Address the agitators.**
5. **Praise the progress.**

The five principles emerge from our experiences and work with leaders and organizations undergoing change. Transformational change within organizations offers HR professionals a wonderful opportunity to become true business partners with the leaders and invaluable wisdom guides to the people within the organization. It is critical that you influence others to promote the benefits of change so that people will persist through all the potholes, detours, obstacles and wrong turns along that change pathway. Let's explore each of the five principles and then see how they operated in two different change scenarios.

Paint the Possibilities

At the start of a change initiative, people view the situation from their own perspectives, based on their limited knowledge and experiences. As such, most members of the organization tend to perceive the changes in a negative light. They have become accustomed to the way things have been, and they anticipate that the positive aspects of their current roles will likely diminish with the change. The greatest need, then, within the organization is to powerfully describe the future after the change, spelling out the array of possibilities. True change only happens from within, and people must see something in another way if they are to act differently. Painting the possibilities means communicating in a variety of ways to help people see and understand a future they have not yet experienced. It offers HR professionals an opportunity to structure formal communications to highlight possible benefits, anticipate possible negatives and offer processes that will help maximize the positives and minimize the negatives of the change initiative.

While it is natural to want to tell people what you think about the change, how you believe the organization will improve as a result and why you feel so strongly about the need for it, you will gain a greater level of commitment by asking people questions such as: *What would it be like if we changed that? What do you think we need to do differently to be more effective? How would that help us? What have you seen or read about that could benefit our organization?* Through the process of answering these questions, people become more aware of what is happening around them, more attentive to your message and more interested in offering their perspectives. HR professionals must recognize the importance of a communication strategy that provides repetitive content messages delivered through multiple media. Since cynics have the past on their side ("This is just another program of the month, another change that won't stick"), you have to invite people to participate by engaging their imaginations. Painting the possibilities helps them take a walk into the future. By seeking out information from other companies that have undergone similar changes, HR professionals are in a position to integrate these companies' experiences in order to persuasively describe the rationale and need for the change and to share stories that will generate a more hopeful view of the future.

As a change agent, you want to focus on winning people's hearts for the change; that is where their commitment lies.

HR professionals also need to create a series of informal information exchanges between employees at all levels and various leaders so that the leaders are regularly painting the possibilities, listening to reactions and providing input to guide formal follow-up communications.

As a change agent, you want to focus on winning people's hearts for the change; that is where their commitment lies. For a change to work, mere compliance is not enough. You also want to concentrate on engaging people's minds to discover the ways they need to change; their minds are where creativity lies. You need them to use their imaginations and creativity to create a better way. Be a painter of possibilities and you will influence everyone's efforts to ensure a successful change.

Increase the Involvement

Since change ends up affecting everyone in an organization in some way, it is essential to earn the commitment of people at various levels and engage them in resolving problems and addressing opportunities during the change process. People are more committed to that which they help shape and create. So many business leaders fall into the trap of thinking, "We'll involve more people once we figure it out." It is a myth that leaders know best. The greatest leaders know that a change is necessary based on the information they have gathered from customers, employees, suppliers, futurists and other leaders in their area and industry. HR professionals keep leaders' attention focused on what changes are needed. You also increase the involvement of others to discover the right process for the change, modifying or shaping the change direction along the way. Be less focused on having the right answer now; instead, become the champion of involving different people at each step of the change process. At the beginning of a change process, there is so much that you cannot know yet. When you involve others, you all embark on a journey of discovery together. Keep the questions flowing: *How would we do that? How could we shift work to free up resources and gather needed information? What anxieties are people expressing around the office, plant, or department? How could we involve other people in this change process?* As involvement increases, so does commitment to making the resulting change work.

Lead the Learning

In order to lead the learning, HR professionals first must get outside their organizations and become avid learners of what is working in other companies. This means that you need to attend conferences, industry association meetings, seminars, workshops and/or classes. You also must voraciously read business magazines, newspapers and journals. By actively gathering information about effective strategies for people in your business, you take the first step in bringing this principle to life. Secondly, you must acknowledge that you do not have answers to many (most) of the questions that come hurtling at you during the early phases of a change initiative, which is perhaps the most difficult aspect of spearheading change or being a change agent. You find it uncomfortable to admit that you do not know; it feels like dodging the issue to respond, "We will discover that answer together." Instead, HR professionals need to lead the learning. In response to such questions, share one of your learning stories. Such stories might begin with, "In a similar situation, we thought ___ and then discovered ___ " or "A colleague of mine shared a story about a similar change effort."

The importance of this principle cannot be overemphasized. An organization is composed of a group of people, and, just like an individual, it develops its habits over time. Once the habits are ingrained, the reasons behind the habits get lost. In organizations, the habits get passed down to successive groups of newcomers with wonderful phrases like, "That is not the way we do it here" or "You need to be here longer before you can make recommendations based on a real understanding of our business." In order to develop new habits, the people inside an organization have to understand the rationale for change and must be willing to discover and learn what the implications are for changed behaviors. The old adage "You can lead a horse to water, but you can't make it drink" is applicable to change initiatives: HR professionals must be adept at making people thirsty for learning. As people acquire new knowledge, they develop better insights that lead to new ways of learning.

The old adage "You can lead a horse to water, but you can't make it drink" is applicable to change initiatives: HR professionals must be adept at making people thirsty for learning.

The third and final aspect of this principle is to create learning groups that are cross-sections of the organization. Some groups need to be more horizontal to address interdepartmental or cross-functional issues. Other groups need to be more vertical to break down the barriers among hierarchical levels. In such learning groups, guiding principles must establish an environment in which people feel safe in honestly sharing their thoughts; these guidelines will reinforce respect for others by encouraging listening to understand, not listening to argue or rebut the speaker's point. The principles must also include a shared accountability for actions that the group will take and support. By taking the lead in the learning process, HR professionals model the courage that others will need in order to accelerate the learning that is essential to a successful change initiative.

Address the Agitators

People's reactions to changes within organizations span a continuum, from strongly opposed to strongly supportive. Since a change agent's goal is to influence people to commit to the change process, you need to know where people are on that continuum in order to develop the necessary strategies for individuals within each group.

While you may enjoy being involved with the supporters of change and may feel stimulated by the interaction clearly aimed at making the change initiative work, HR professionals must take a proactive stance in dealing effectively and early in the process with those who oppose the change. Fortunately, you should be most concerned with those who will attempt to influence others to resist the change with them; these people are the agitators.

Addressing the agitators is a direct approach that has three possible outcomes. The first, and best, outcome is to convert agitators into change agents. With their skills of persuasion and newfound passion for the change, such converts can have a much greater impact on the organization than the people who were always change agents could. Converts understand the opposition and can share their reasons for their switch in thinking. Change agents, on the other hand, often are dismissed by others because "they always see through rose-colored glasses" or "they always support what management says." The second, and neutral, outcome is to have agitators shift to a passive role: Even if they still oppose a change, they will keep their discontent to themselves. This result minimizes the disruptions to the change initiatives that active agitators can cause. The third outcome is essential and at some point must be made clear to the individual agitators: They must know that if they cannot either support the change initiative or remain passive in their opposition, they must leave the organization. Agitators are like a cancer that infects the group; as opposition grows, it kills the change initiative and leaves the organization in an even weaker condition.

As a change agent, HR professionals can neither ignore the agitators nor take a subtle approach to them. Invite agitators into the process, actively encourage their input, and freely share information and progress. These steps will most likely lead to conversion. As the initiative progresses and opposition deepens, it is incumbent upon the HR professional to confront agitators about the second and third options. If it would be more effective from an organizational standpoint for another leader to address the problem, feel free to handle it that way. Addressing the agitators will be a true challenge, but the payoff for handling it well is enormous.

Praise the Progress

In the midst of a change initiative, people become most aware of what is not working. They experience frustration, irritation, confusion or any number of other emotions that sap energy, demoralize and anger group members, and diminish any remaining optimism about the results of the changes. As much as you plan, design and adjust a change initiative, you will still encounter unexpected incidents, unfortunate missteps and numerous obstacles. To counteract the natural reactions to adversity and deal with the unexpected yet inevitable negative occurrences, the change agent must make the "praise the progress" principle a regular—weekly, or even daily—mantra. You need to create multiple definitions of progress and then convey this progress to others by several methods, recording it in visible places.

How do you define progress? Here are a few examples that should give you a good idea:

- The confirmation of a cross-sectional group
- The conflicting perspectives at a learning session that illustrate the necessity of doing the work to get everyone on the same page
- The change in an approach upon discovering that it will not solve the redefined issue
- An agreement to create a small, cross-functional work group that will develop a priority list of issues causing conflict

By defining progress as any step forward, redirection that will prevent further backsliding or agreement that creates a point from which the organization can move forward, the HR professional provides the organization with a way to emphasize the development of the change initiative. Much like planting a seed, the early progress (growth) takes place out of sight (like roots underground), but it is essential to a successful outcome (because a weak root system limits growth).

The HR professional's expertise in praising enables this principle to flourish. Capture progress comments that others are making and create a quick story for an e-mail, bulletin board, newsletter or informal talk with leaders. Measure efforts and progress using realistic benchmarks from other change experiences; do not just use the change plan, which is too often unrealistic. Build progress visuals and visible scorecards so the good aspects of the change will be in sight and in mind. As you praise the progress, you are adding real energy to the organization and providing fuel that people need to persevere.

Two Change Scenarios

The following change scenarios have the following factors in common:

- An internal HR leader and an external lead consultant working in partnership. To make true change occur, this partnership must be collaborative and based on mutual respect. Each person brings essential experience to the table that is necessary for success; neither one has all the ingredients.

- A leadership team assembled to accelerate change within the organization.

- An organization facing significant pressure to increase profitability while substantially redesigning and reconfiguring the organizational structure.

1) An Enterprise-Wide Change Initiative

A financial services company was planning to make the shift from private ownership by policyholders to public ownership. The vice-president of HR was charged with creating a change initiative that, in just nine months, would educate more than 55,000 employees about why the change in ownership structure was necessary, what internal changes had to occur as a result and how the company was responding to the changing competitive marketplace. Recognizing the enormous logistical challenge and understanding the principles of adult education, the VP of HR melded the expertise of facilitating large-scale community meetings and the use of learning maps (with which a previous employer had experimented). The intervention design used a cascading approach. The first community meeting was the leadership launch with the Chief Executive Officer and the top 125 leaders in the organization. The day-long meeting started with the CEO's opening comments about the company's strategic plan and the critical role that this intervention would play in reaching every person within the enterprise. The leaders then experienced the three learning maps:

The Changing Marketplace

How the Company Makes Money

The Strategic Responses Underway

The meeting was facilitated by two external consultants, and the leaders were divided among fourteen tables; a table coach (a consultant with the large-scale change firm) guided the learning map process for each group of leaders. At the end of the program, leaders were asked to choose a partner from a different part of the company and sign up to lead several sets of community meetings around the country. Each pair of leaders would provide the opening comments for these day-long meetings of up to 300 people from across the company. The consulting firm videotaped the leadership launch and collected videotaped comments from the CEO and various leaders about the change initiative and their reactions to the community meeting and learning maps. From this footage, the consultants created a twenty-minute video to be used at all subsequent community meetings. The second set of meetings was to prepare managers from throughout the company to serve as table coaches. A pair of leaders from the launch session gave their opening comments and showed the video, the managers experienced the three learning maps (with the external consultants as table coaches), and the leader pair provided an inspirational wrap-up.

As the community meetings were held (with a leader pair opening and closing, managers as table coaches and two consultants as meeting facilitators), the company's project director and project team met monthly with the consulting firm's facilitators and designers to exchange information and review key lessons. These meetings created a safe environment, and the perspectives shared were refreshingly frank. In order to measure the impact of the meetings, the company added a demographic item to its quarterly employee survey that distinguished employees who had attended a community meeting from those who had not yet done so. The consulting firm also set up video kiosks where employees could provide comments or pose questions. The consultants compiled the video footage and showed it to the leadership group during their periodic meetings. The meeting facilitators and the leadership pairs worked as a collaborative team during the community meetings, and their combined expertise enabled them to defuse the hostility of some participants and to underscore the need for embracing the change.

After members of a work group had all attended a community meeting, the group leader held a work group action meeting to generate changes at the local level that would be consistent with the directional changes shared at the community meetings. The work group meetings were audited by the consulting firm, and the group leaders prepared a summary of the meeting with thirty-, sixty- and ninety-day timetables of actions; one of the top 125 leaders received each of these work group reports. From the external consultant audits and the group reports, leaders selected progress anecdotes for broader communication and identified new initiatives that were added to later community meetings. The consulting firm helped the company create a feedback-rich environment and measure progress through methods like the employee survey.

2) Shift from a Service Bureau Technology Provider to a Technology Outsourcing Company

The HR leader of the services division of a technology conglomerate recognized the need for a transformational change that would require adding several employees with different skill sets, which could cause many of the company's existing personnel to either rapidly develop new skills or leave the organization. The change challenge was to redesign the organization from an account manager/client technology leader interface to a system in which an account team interacted with the client counterpart in a true outsourcing framework. The HR leader also needed to work with existing personnel to revamp their career development plans and had to accelerate the integration of new personnel into the organization.

The design of the intervention included career-development workshops coupled with supervisor/manager-as-coach workshops; focus groups to address new personnel integration issues; and a series of meetings of forty-five executives, directors and managers with key roles in securing new clients and implementing the outsource agreement. The company had added its first full outsourcing contract the previous year, and several subsequent clients had complained about how long it took the company to get the clients' systems switched to company management. The HR leader engaged a consulting group with career-development expertise and had them hire a training leader to serve as the training champion, working with the company's newly-formed training task force. When the new client issues cropped up, the HR leader asked the consultants if they could help. The consultants admitted that this would be a new area for them, to which the HR leader responded, "Let's learn together and create some good history." This collaborative team approach became a key factor in the change initiative's success.

As existing personnel pursued and obtained new opportunities, the leader broadly communicated the changes, whether the new positions were within the division, within the corporation or outside of the organization. He attended the new coaching workshop and influenced most of the functional directors to also attend. While the sessions were facilitated by an external consultant, the follow-up to the session was integrated into the company's performance-management process. The new client issue was addressed through a process coined as the 3-D Initiative (Design of the contract, Development of the needed infrastructure, Delivery of the services). The executive VP, the lead consultant and the HR leader collaborated in selecting the forty-five people to participate. The HR leader was one of the participants and guided the outside consultant in creating the interactive subgroups needed for the process. Included in the group of forty-five were a number of outspoken managers who generally resisted change. These managers were distributed among the subgroups so that they expressed their opinions but did not dominate discussions. At the end of the two-month process, the 3-D group had created a SWAT team to work with selected new clients; the team was able to bring the clients on board within forty-five days, as opposed to the usual 150 days that it might have taken with the old process. The approach was so successful that the company decided to restructure along the SWAT team format.

Navigating the Challenge of Change

The HR leaders in these two examples became adept at utilizing the five principles:

Paint the possibilities: Understanding the trends affecting their respective businesses helped these HR leaders position the change initiatives as an integral part of the overall strategic plan and not just an HR program.

Increase the involvement: The situations described occurred while the organizations were under intense pressure to increase profit margins. Yet the leaders were able to underscore that these initiatives were investments that would add to the revenue line and, through heightened awareness of spending patterns, would also lead to better management of expenditures.

Lead the learning: These HR leaders were able to model learning through their own involvement and the involvement of the business leaders. Other members of the organizations had a greater desire to commit to learning when they witnessed their leaders acknowledging the new insights they had gained through the change initiative.

Address the agitators: In each situation, the initiatives were designed to strategically include strong-willed, outspoken opponents of the change initiative. There were a good number of key converts; most of the rest of the agitators became passive about the change, and some chose to leave when they saw that continued active opposition was not an option.

Praise the progress: Throughout the change initiatives, these HR leaders created information-rich environments. They worked with their corporate communications departments and the external consultants to identify content, reinforce messages, share success anecdotes and create multiple feedback loops. Front-line employees had the chance to interact with top executives. These interchanges accelerated improvements throughout the organizations and gave the executives a much more realistic view of the organizations' interaction with customers.

Embrace these five principles and apply them to your own change situation. With practice and persistence, you will become a master navigator of change.

About The Author

George Ritcheske

George has over 25 years experience in leadership development processes with international professional service firms, as well as energy, telecommunications, high tech, and hospitality organizations. He works with leaders in enhancing their effectiveness and the effectiveness of their teams, utilizing 360-degree feedback processes, assessments, and organization-wide communication processes. George facilitates exceptional retreats for strategic planning and implementation, as well as leadership team development and structured offsites for business problem resolution. As a professional speaker and workshop leader, George addresses such topics as True Leadership; The Challenge of Change; True Team Building; The Manager as Teacher, Leader, Coach; and The Power of Differences. George is the co-author of the book *True Leaders: How Exceptional CEOs and Presidents Make A Difference by Building People and Profits* (Dearborn Publishing, December 2001), which presents 10 leadership principles drawn from interviews with 27 CEOs and Presidents. He earned his B.A. in Economics at Dartmouth College and his M.B.A. at the University of Michigan. He is a member of the International Coach Federation, the Organization Development Network, and the National Speakers Association. He has been actively involved in community organizations, including the Boy Scouts of America and Rotary International.

George Ritcheske, President
TrueLeaderCoach, Inc.
5215 N. O'Connor Blvd., Suite 200
Irving, TX 75039
Tel: 972-304-6137
Fax: 214-722-2344
Email: george@trueleadercoach.com
Website: www.trueleadercoach.com

Chapter Nine

Sales Excellence And The HR Professional

Richard Tyler

"It's not our fault." "We did the best we could do." "The company simply had other priorities. . ."

Ever find yourself delivering that familiar speech to your team? You know—the one that seems to follow every budget-planning season, the one that will mark yet one more year where the HR programs that everyone demands but no one supports get pushed to "next year" because of "budget constraints."

If you can identify with this theme, then I have some very excellent news for you. After reading this chapter, you will have the tools you need to turn "next year" into NOW. How can I be so confident? Because I have discovered a *secret*. A *secret* that most people do not know. A *secret* that, once understood and combined with an attitude of excellence, *always* gets results.

What is this magical *secret*? Simply stated, **the approval of your HR programs or initiatives has nothing to do with your company's budget!** Once you understand this truth and its implications, you will begin to unlock amazing opportunities for you and your company. We will discuss this in detail later in the chapter. But first, we must address the second critical element to achieving success: adopting an attitude of excellence.

The truth is no one stumbles into excellence; it is something that is achieved only after there is a commitment, a mental determination to accept *only* excellence, no matter how difficult, no matter how uncomfortable and no matter how stressful the journey may be. As your company's HR professional, you are in a position of access and trust—unlike any other position; you have access to every function in your company. It doesn't matter if your company builds cars or prepares tax returns. You touch everyone in your organization. And whether or not you realize it, everyone watches what you say and do. Everyone assumes you know what's going on in the company, because you regularly interact with all departments as well as senior management (never mind the reality that HR is too often the last to know!).

Most HR professionals who have been in the business for even a short time understand that their actions are often interpreted as signals for some decision that "the company" has made or is contemplating. If you understand this, then you also understand how valuable establishing trust is to forming great relationships. Without trust, it's easy for employees to begin viewing the HR team as spies or simply rule enforcers.

The HR professional committed to excellence uses access to build rapport, establishes trust and develops long-term partnerships. These partnerships serve as the foundation for establishing the company's commitment to HR programs—the programs necessary for the company to achieve excellence in business.

In this chapter, we will review the techniques necessary for the HR professional to achieve excellence. We will also provide step-by-step guidance to leveraging "*the secret.*" As you will soon see, the HR professional is just as much in the *sales business* as any salesperson charged with selling a company's products or services. There is great power in that realization. But this information is *not* power. It is *potential* power. Only information put to use is real power. If you commit to putting the techniques outlined in this chapter to work, you will be well on your way to achieving your goals faster than you have imagined. Let's get started with a true story that will help illustrate some key points.

If you commit to using the "Tyler 4" ™
Fundamentals ™, you *will* get results!

Craig was the HR director for a Fortune 500 corporation that was in need of management talent. He had an excellent idea for an updated HR system, one that would be integrated with the basic HR software and would also track the training and development of each employee. It would identify "rising stars" and personalize a development plan for those with management potential. Craig went to each department head to tell them about his new idea. Everyone seemed to agree that this would be helpful, and Craig quickly submitted this program as the centerpiece of his budget.

Just as quickly, however, Craig's program was cut from the budget. In fact, the same department heads that seemed to agree that the program was a good idea were the ones to cut it from the budget—almost immediately. Searching for answers, Craig approached one department head.

"It sounded like a good idea, Craig, but no one felt that it would generate revenue or reduce costs, and we were in a crunch!"

Craig was shocked. "This program was designed to reduce turnover and save the company a great deal of expense. A manager promoted from within the company would be up to speed much faster as a new recruit. And think of the morale boost in seeing real growth opportunity. How could they not see this?"

Over the course of many years of research, practice and refinement, I have developed highly effective sales techniques and methodologies. The foundation of these sales techniques is the **"Tyler 4"™ Fundamentals™**. Once you understand and begin practicing these fundamentals in your business, you will be able to lead your company's (or client's) decision makers to positive investment decisions in the right HR initiatives. This approach is straight forward, easy to learn and flexible. Most importantly, if you commit to using it, you *will* get results.

The Tyler 4™ Fundamental #1: RAPPORT BUILDING

In most organizations, you can hear the familiar refrain: "Those HR folks just don't understand us! They are always proposing programs that are expensive and impractical. They may look good on paper, but they just won't work in the real world."

Before you can sell that great new idea that will result in more productive employees, lower expenses and higher revenues, you must build a lasting rapport with the decision makers in your organization. You might ask, "Why? Why can't I just tell them about the benefits of the new program? Can't they see what's good for them?" Well, the answer is no—at least not the way you are presenting it. It's not that the people in your organization have no idea about what's best for their department. Rather, they just don't trust that *you* know what's best, and so they are skeptical of anything you are "pushing."

By building rapport, you will be establishing a relationship of trust. That trust then leads to a partnership between HR and the other departments in your organization. With the right rapport, you will form the foundation for discerning each department's wants and needs.

It's easy to skip over this section and say, "Yeah, yeah, I know all about rapport building; after all, I'm an HR professional!" I agree that successful HR professionals are, generally speaking, good at rapport building; however, because of the significant hurdles you face in getting agreement on programs and initiatives, you can't settle for just being good. You must become an expert. Take the time to carefully review the six simple yet essential components to building rapport. Find ways to improve your rapport-building skills and then practice. I guarantee your efforts will pay off.

Throughout the rest of what you read, you will see that I often refer to the people that you have day-to-day interactions with as your *customers*. I am doing this because at every turn, I want to remind you that they are truly your *customers*. You are selling many items— ideas, programs and solutions, to name just a few. You have to assist your *customers* in making decisions to invest their time and/or money in these items. When you stay focused on these interactions as needing to be *customer* focused, you will have improved results.

Look professional

Do not underestimate the power of looking professional. Studies consistently demonstrate that those who appear more professional are taken more seriously and achieve greater results. This doesn't mean you have to wear a formal business suit every day; you must dress in a way that makes sense for your environment. Even if your company's dress code is business casual, resist the temptation to wear a golf shirt and khakis. If instead you wear a nicely pressed white blouse or shirt and suit pants, you will be dressing within the company's guidelines while sending a subtle (but strong) message that you are serious about what you do. The simple truth is that a professional appearance *does* make a difference, and it is a big difference.

Smile

It doesn't cost a thing, and yet it delivers huge benefits when developing a good relationship. As motivational speaker Les Giblin said, *"If you're not using your smile, you're like a man with a million dollars in the bank and no checkbook."* A smile shows that you are caring, concerned and candid with everyone.

Make eye contact

Making and maintaining eye contact shows that you have a genuine interest in the person with whom you are engaged. Your eye contact sends a very powerful message: "You are important, and I am genuinely interested and concerned about what you are saying." Maintaining eye contact will also help you remain in control. By conveying the message that "I'm listening to everything you say. I'm interested in you and your ideas," *you earn the right to change the course of the conversation.* Let me give you an example. In the following dialogue between an HR manager and a plant manager, assume that the HR manager has been actively listening to the plant manager for five minutes. Watch how the HR manager changes the course of the dialogue:

Plant manager:	" . . . and now it's been three weeks of below-standard performance."
HR manager:	"Jim, I want to make sure I understand what you're saying, because I believe you have some really key insights here. If I understand you correctly, you're saying that production is suffering because every time you lose an employee, you have to start from scratch, recruiting and training a new employee. And this drops production below acceptable levels."
Plant manager:	"Yes, Cindy, that's exactly right. And I really don't know if there is anything we can do about it."
HR manager:	"Well, Jim, you've already given me an idea. You said that the only thing that keeps you afloat is that you can usually get some of the experienced employees to cover for the open position. Is that correct?
Plant manager:	"Yes."

```
HR manager:            "What if we worked together to create a
                       formal cross-training program? It would
                       certainly give us greater continuity when
                       we have an opening, and it might even
                       boost morale and help increase our reten-
                       tion rate."
```

Because the HR manager in this example was using eye contact and active listening to demonstrate interest in the plant manager's challenges, she had license to change the course of the conversation and get involved with the plant manager to create solutions. She came to the plant manager that morning to get him to approve a new cross-training plan. If she had just walked into his office and said, "Jim, we need to implement the X2000 cross-training system," he would have likely said something like, "How about if you get me some people that will stay around first? It's hard to implement a training program if no one stays around long enough to complete it." Sound familiar? By using eye contact and active listening skills, Cindy established trust and turned a complaint into a dialogue seeking to solve a challenge.

Use icebreakers

Ask about your *customers'* families or about hobbies or interests that you know they have. Most people see HR as the department you call when you have problems or need to fire someone, so helping people relax is key to building a good rapport. Share a story that shows you understand the challenges a person is facing. Use humor to engage your *customer's* interest. A simple, effective icebreaker can be asking for some simple help with a problem in that persons area of expertise—one that isn't time consuming but allows them to demonstrate their knowledge.

Be confident

Confidence begets confidence. If you want to earn others' confidence, you have to demonstrate confidence. You are the HR expert—and you have services and products that will help the leaders in your company do their jobs better. But you will not be taken seriously if you are not confident in your capabilities. Objectively evaluate your strengths and weaknesses. Write them down. Then create a plan of action to improve your weaknesses and leverage your strengths. For example, if a weakness is lack of in-depth knowledge of an area of your company, commit to spending at least a portion of every week for the next four to six weeks learning the details. Your interest in the area and contact with the members of that department will go along way toward helping you establish rapport and trust.

"Sincerity if the highest compliment you can pay."
- Ralph Waldo Emerson

Be sincere

Your genuine interest in the cares and concerns of each area of your company is the key to providing the best HR service that you can. Asking your *customers* open-ended questions about their departments allows them more opportunity to discuss what is important to them and helps you gather vital information for the **Wants and Needs Analysis™.**

You should also assume that the other person thinks you have some hidden agenda. You are probably well aware of this negative bias that HR professionals face. Anticipating it will help you ease the other person's mind and allow you to more quickly establish a trust relationship.

The Tyler 4™ Fundamental #2: WANTS AND NEEDS ANALYSIS™

A Wants and Needs Analysis™ is the actual determination of your customer's wants and needs through the use of probing questions. Find out what is happening in the company and what your *customer* thinks should be happening. It is this gap between *what is* and *what should be* that will be the motivation for investing in your ideas.

The keys to effectively understanding what is important to your customer are excellent planning and communication.

PLANNING

A friend of mine once told me that an attorney he knows shared one of his success secrets: When the attorney was preparing for a trial, he would repeat to himself every day, "He who is most prepared wins." The attorney was convinced that his successful litigation record was not the result of being the most intelligent or having the best set of facts; he believed he was successful because he was simply better prepared than the other side.

Get to know as much about your *customers* as possible. Where did they work before coming to your company? In what other areas do they have experience? What is their record of attainment or success? Have they won any industry or company awards? As an HR professional, you are knowledgeable about your company, so now is the time to get to know this specific area more thoroughly. Study all the relevant information that you can find. This is easier if you are an internal HR professional rather than a consultant. However, even if you are outside of the company, there will be a great deal of available information through public databases and trusted contacts.

Memorize your questions. Practice them with a colleague until they are second nature to you. Use your questions to lead your *customers* into a discussion of what is important to them regarding the proposal you are developing. Where is their pain? What would bring them the most reward? How does your HR initiative fit?

I had an HR professional tell me, "My company has a very high employee turnover rate in a few areas. How do I convince the managers of the low-turnover areas to invest in a program designed to reduce turnover? They tell me there's nothing in it for them."

I asked him, "What is the turnover rate in accounting?" He said it had one of the highest turnover rates.

I said, "Aren't the low-turnover departments affected by accounting's high turnover?"

"Aha!" A light bulb flashed, and he understood instantly. The high employee turnover was clearly a challenge for everyone. By asking probing questions and illustrating the impact of high turnover, even in a few areas, he established the need for the initiative.

Plan each part of your meeting. Your *customers* are busy people, just like you, and their time is limited. A well-planned meeting will allow you to gather the information you need while respecting the participants' time.

COMMUNICATION

Communication is the key to every successful relationship, and selling is all about developing lasting relationships. An excellent communicator is an active listener. Being an active listener will help you to develop rapport, gather information and achieve positive investment decisions in your HR initiatives. An active listener is one that uses all of his or her senses to focus and fully engage in the conversation and to lead the conversation where it needs to go. If you commit to practicing the following principles, you will become an excellent communicator.

Be attentive to the person

This means being focused and relaxed. As an HR professional, it may be easier to be focused if you are meeting in a neutral place, away from phones and staff that might draw your attention away from your *customer*. The average person speaks about 150 words per minute, and the average listener can process 500 words per minute. This means it takes significant effort to remain focused when someone is speaking. In order to remain focused, practice this simple and easy technique. Look the person in the eye and repeat in your mind what is being said.

Ask open-ended questions

An open-ended question is any question that cannot be answered with a simple yes or no. An open-ended question starts with who, what, when, where, why or how. Closed-ended questions are questions that are answered with a yes or a no. Asking open-ended questions shows interest, helps you gather information and determines your *customer's* values, philosophies, principles and beliefs. Most importantly, asking your *customers* open-ended questions will help you understand their investment motives; what they think is the most compelling reason to invest in your HR initiative. It could be to increase profits, to hold back costs, to be a more effective and recognized leader in the company or perhaps to provide for their employees and have a more stable workforce.

When you ask open-ended questions, be sure that you are:

> *Sincere*
> *Confident*
> *Clear*
> *Creative*
> *Logical*
> *Consistent*

Understand and be aware of body language

Nod, laugh, smile, show concern, use appropriate posture and be aware of your facial expressions. At the same time, be aware of your *customer's* body language. Peter Drucker once stated, "The most important thing in communication is to hear what isn't being said." Does your *customer* make eye contact, smile or nod when you speak? What are his or her movements telling you? Look for clues. If your *customer* is relaxed, you can move on to gathering information. If not, then continue your rapport-building techniques.

Show vulnerability

Another key to excellent communication is being honest about what you *don't* know. This shows that you are vulnerable and in turn will help your *customer* to be more comfortable about your integrity. It is also a great way to gather information, as the decision maker now has the opportunity to share knowledge.

Use feedback

Finally, feedback is crucial to excellent communication. Use interest statements like "Is that right?" or "That is exciting!" or "I am so sorry to hear that" to demonstrate that you are listening and are empathetic.

It is often effective to repeat a portion of what the person has said: "Joe, it is so exciting that your area has the lowest turnover rate in the company!" This shows that you are listening and that you are responding or reacting appropriately to what he is saying. Wait for a pause to interject these interest statements so that you never talk over your *customer*. Use feedback to ensure you have an understanding of what is being said and to gain agreement. You could say something like, "Let me make sure I understand you…" and then give your interpretation of what was being said.

It is also a good idea to take notes to make sure of capturing the important information. When you do, use a professional pad, not scraps of paper. It will be a great memory aid, and it will demonstrate that what the *customer* is saying is very important to you. Once you have a clear understanding of the wants and needs of your *customer*, you are ready to discuss the HR product or service that would benefit him or her.

The Tyler 4™ Fundamental #3: Product Knowledge

Once you have established rapport—a relationship of trust—and you have worked to understand your customer's wants and needs, you need to make sure you have complete product knowledge. Product knowledge is the necessary information (features and facts) needed to direct your customer to the most appropriate HR initiative. Use the following points to assist you:

- Present the features and advantages of your HR initiative in terms of how the initiative will meet your *customer's* wants and needs.

- Make clear the benefits to your *customer's* area of the company as well as to the company as a whole.

- When developing your **Presentation/Demonstration™**, be sure to include information about industry trends, competitive facts, latest technology, market conditions and return on investment.

- Compare the current system or service with the one you are proposing.

- Include a comparison with similar products or services on a fact sheet.

- Whenever possible, demonstrate how other organizations or companies that are well respected in your industry are using this HR product or service. Testimonial letters from these companies will be very effective.

- Remember that Presentation/Demonstration™ means having your *customer* hear, see and be involved with what you are covering.

This Presentation/Demonstration™ can be distributed in the form of a professional-looking, bound handout or a projection from a computer using any presentation software. The presentation should capture your *customer's* attention and provide all the key information about the product or idea. You will be presenting this information to various decision makers with different wants and needs, so make sure that the Presentation/Demonstration™ is flexible and modular. That way, it can be easily adapted to different audiences. In other words, don't use the same "canned" presentation for everyone; that won't be nearly as effective!

The answers that you received when doing your Wants-and-Needs Analysis™ will allow you to start your Presentation/Demonstration™. Use this information to be creative and to make your Presentation/Demonstration™ personal and professional.

For example: "Joe, you said you were having trouble finding good managers who understand our company and our business. Is that correct?"

"Yes."

"Well, let me show you how this HR program will solve that problem."

If you have built rapport and used open-ended questions to show your interest and gather information, then the transition to the Presentation/Demonstration™ will be smooth and professional. If not, you may seem pushy or insincere. So be sure to take the time to lay the foundation for this important, fundamental step.

The objective of the Presentation/Demonstration™ is to establish how your HR initiative will provide solutions to your *customers'* challenges, thereby satisfying their wants and needs and leading them to a positive investment decision.

An effective Presentation/Demonstration™ contains two-way communication. Don't talk *at* your *customer*! You are continuing to gather information and secure agreements as you present your information. Look for both verbal and non-verbal communication. Remember: Non-verbal responses or reactions are often more reflective of your customers' true feelings than verbal responses or reactions. What are their facial expressions, body movements, eye contact or state of relaxation/tenseness telling you?

Welcome questions. Questions give you the opportunity to give more information and to gain feedback about the concerns of your *customer*. Questions give you a chance to use **Testers**™. Testers are questions that, when answered, positively give you an indication of a high level of interest and readiness to invest in the HR product you are offering. For example, your *customer* might ask, "How much will this program reduce my turnover?" Your tester question might be, "The data indicate that this program reduces turnover more than any single HR initiative; what would you consider a significant reduction in your employee turnover?"

Address concerns as they come up. In order to overcome concerns, you must learn to uncover the real or underlying message. An example: If your *customer* says or their body language indicates "Slow down," they may mean that you are giving too much information too quickly or that you are being pushy. Get as many positive agreements on specific points throughout your presentation as possible. Get the *customer* comfortable with saying yes.

Many HR professionals make the mistake of stopping with the Presentation/Demonstration™, thinking the *customer* is ready to make a positive investment decision. Remember the example with Craig from earlier in the chapter? Craig's mistake was in thinking that he was developing support for his initiative when all he was doing was conducting a survey. He presented *his* new idea without linking it to the *customers'* wants and needs and without ever establishing a trust relationship. It was easy for the department heads to say, "Sounds like a good idea." Committing to the initiative as a solution to their needs was something entirely different. Craig missed this point, and the result was inevitable.

The Tyler 4™ Fundamental #4: PROFESSIONALISM

Many people in key HR positions believe that their success is based on their knowledge of HR issues. And while a solid knowledge of HR matters is absolutely essential, it is only the beginning. The best HR professionals in the industry understand that to be the best, they must develop a commitment to excellence—a pattern and practice of continuous improvement.

Mastering the first three fundamentals gets you to a new level of effectiveness. Putting it all together is what the fourth fundamental—professionalism—is about. Professionalism is the ability to effectively communicate the features and facts of your HR initiative in terms of the benefits to each area of your company. It is the ability to effectively resolve any concerns that may arise. It's about effectively leading your *customer* to a positive investment decision.

People do not care how much you know until they know how much you care.

Before we go into more detail on professionalism, let's review what we've learned about building rapport, conducting a Wants-and-Needs Analysis™ and developing product knowledge.

We started with building rapport. Rapport building continues throughout the entire "sales" process. Discover and show genuine concern for the business challenges your *customer* is facing. Remember, people do not care how much you know until they know how much you care.

Find out what makes your customers tick. What are their motivations? Think of it as tuning in to their radio station, WIIFM (What's In It For Me?). If you can tune in to that frequency, you will have no problem staying focused on what is important to your *customer*. Keep the information that you learned during your Wants-and-Needs Analysis™ in front of you and use it during the agreement phase. Have the features and facts about your HR initiative memorized, and be completely familiar with all the important data that you have to present.

And now it's time to reach an agreement—time to sell your HR program. Throughout your time with your *customer*, you have been listening to concerns and having the *customer* agree with points throughout your Presentation/Demonstration™. Whenever possible, you have used Testers™ to verify that the customer is moving forward with you in your Presentation/Demonstration™. Before you reach an agreement, you may have to address any lingering customer concerns about the HR initiative.

Be sure to tune into your customer's favorite radio station—WIIFM.

Ask your *customer* if he or she has any questions or concerns about what you have presented. Use Tester™ questions to bring out any concerns or questions. "Joe, would you like me to give you the amount to put in your department's budget for this valuable HR initiative, based on your current number of employees or on your estimated number of employees for the next fiscal year?" This is an example of an **Alternate Option Tester™**. An Alternate Option Tester™ is a question with two self-contained answers, either of which is a positive response to the investment decision. You see in this example that whether the answer is on this year's number of employees or next year's estimated number of employees, the decision is positive for the HR initiative.

If a concern is stated after the Tester™ question, use **The Tyler 6™ Power Resolution Steps**™:

STEP 1: Listen to the concern – Don't interrupt your *customer* before he or she completely expresses the concern. If you do that, you will irritate the person and risk appearing defensive or elusive. You might even be considered pushy or unconcerned. Worst of all, you could address the wrong issue and bring up a concern your *customer* didn't even have (at least until that point!).

STEP 2: Give the concern back – If you repeat the concern back in your own words, you will be able to confirm that you understand the concern fully. You will also show your *customer* that you are sincere about addressing what is important to him or her. The added advantage is that you'll give yourself more time to formulate the right answer.

STEP 3: Investigate the concern – Seriously and sincerely ask your *customer* to explain the concern in more detail. Be sure you understand exactly what want or need is not being met. Ask open-ended probing questions. This will create a desire on the part of your *customer* to remove the concern himself if it is not too serious. If your customer does not remove it, this will still give you more time to decide on the correct solution.

STEP 4: Resolve the concern – Use your skills, product knowledge and knowledge of your *customer's* wants and needs to gain agreement on a solution that *will* work for both you and your *customer*. It's important to remember that every initiative is not perfect and will invariably have some weak points. Just handle them when they arise by admitting the weakness and then overpowering that weakness with the advantages your HR initiative offers. After all, you wouldn't be proposing it if you didn't think it was the best available solution for your *customer*. The *customer* needs that reassurance.

STEP 5: Verify the answer – Ask your *customer* to verify that he or she heard your solution and understands how it answers the concern. This can be done with a statement like "Mary, doesn't this explanation satisfy the concern you have?" Make sure you reach agreement that you have resolved the concern before going further.

STEP 6: Disengage – Once you have agreement that the concern is resolved, leave that concern and indicate to your *customer* that you are moving forward. You can do this both verbally ("Let me show you…") and non-verbally (shifting your body, moving your paperwork, etc.). **Knowing when to stop talking is just as important as knowing when to start.**

How do you know when your *customer* is ready to make an agreement? There are some easy-to-read signs. For example, when the person begins to ask more questions, it usually means he or she is more engaged and interested. Often, your *customer* will ask for more technical data, indicating a more in-depth interest level. A sure-fire indicator is when your *customer* starts to talk about post-implementation stages—that is, how he or she will be using or bene-fiting from the initiative. Now the *customer* is imagining his or her life made easier with your initiative. Also, watch for non-verbal signs such as smiling or even excitement. And if the *customer* asks to see the Presentation/Demonstration™ again, by all means show it!

When the customer begins to ask more questions, it usually means he or she is very interested.

The goal of a traditional salesperson is to reach agreement and do it quickly (the shorter the sales cycle the better). For this reason, the excellent salesperson keeps a wide variety of agreement methods at hand.(Remember, as an HR professional you are in sales) There are many different methods; you should be familiar with at least a few of them and be prepared to use them. Let's review a few that will be invaluable additions to your excellence toolkit.

Basic Oral Agreement – Any simple question or statement that asks your *customer* to make an investment decision is a Basic Oral Agreement. You can ask, "What purchase order will be assigned to this?" Another such question is, "Would you fill out this budget request form?"

Sharp Angle Agreement – or "If I could, would you" agreement. Your *customer* says, "If we went with this HR program, could I pick the people that would be using this system from my area?" Your response is, "If I could guarantee that you would be in charge of selecting the users, would you be ready to approve this new program today?"

Limited Time Agreement – This is an urgency agreement. As an HR professional, you have experienced times when you can offer a new program at an affordable investment but only if it can be approved quickly. "Joe, we can get this excellent new benefit package if we are ready to move on it immediately. Can I get your approval today so that our employees can begin taking advantage of all that it has to offer them?"

Feel, Felt, Found Agreement – This agreement is based on you showing empathy to your *customer*. You state that you understand their feelings. That you or someone else found out a solution that allowed you or someone else to change their mind. Using the exact words "feel" "felt" and "found" is very important here. For example: "Joe, I can understand how you **feel** about the investment for this HR initiative. Alecia in accounting **felt** the same way that you do until she **found** out that the program will pay for itself by reducing turnover by just five percent. Lowering turnover costs would help you too, wouldn't it?"

Conditional Agreement – This agreement is used whenever a condition exists that is blocking the sale from moving forward.

Department Head:	"We can't approve this, because our budget hasn't been approved yet."
HR Professional:	"So Joe, if I understand you correctly, you like this HR program and want to go ahead with it; however, you need to get your budget approved. Is that correct?"
Department Head:	"Yes."
HR Professional:	"Excellent. I will just write up the request for this new program with the condition that your budget must be approved in order for it to be valid. Now that solves the situation, doesn't it?"
Department Head:	"Yes."
HR Professional:	"I just need your autograph right here on my paperwork to confirm this agreement."

Three Simple Questions Agreement – This simple agreement method is used whenever you can demonstrate that a product or service will improve something for your *customer*.

HR Professional: "Can you see how this new program will
                     reduce expenses?"
Department Head: "Yes."
HR Professional: "Are you interested in lowering costs in
                     your area?"
Department Head: "Yes."
HR Professional: "When would be a good time to start
                     lowering costs for the company?"
Department Head: "As soon as possible!"

These are just a few of the many excellent sales-agreement strategies that are available to the HR professional who is interested in selling an idea or product. Commit them to memory and practice them. I assure you they will make you more successful at achieving your goals.

Remember each *customer* is an individual. So personalize your use of **"The Tyler 4"**™ **Fundamentals™**. Commit your Presentation/Demonstration™ to memory. The more you practice, the more effortless it will seem to your *customer* and the more confidence your *customer* will have in your information, your Presentation/Demonstration™ and you as a partner. A well-practiced Presentation/Demonstration™ will speed up the sales process and guarantee you a successful result.

Once you have reached agreement on your HR initiative, your work is not complete. Follow-through is an important part of the sales process. Verify that your *customer* is satisfied. Measure the success of your new HR program. Provide instruction and *customer service* to ensure that your program is well utilized. A satisfied *customer* in one area of the company will be your best ally for achieving success with other areas of the company.

Remember the *secret* that we discussed at the beginning of this chapter? Wouldn't you now agree with me that the approval of your HR programs or initiative has nothing to do with your company's budget? The "budget" is an easy excuse. The truth is that if the HR initiative is going to satisfy key wants and needs necessary for your organization to reach its goals, then the annual budget has nothing to do with whether your initiative gets approved. What *does* matter is how well you are able to implement **"The Tyler 4"™ Fundamentals™** sales techniques.

How would Craig's experience have been different had he mastered "TheTyler 4"™ Fundamentals™?

Let's imagine Craig's experience the following year after implementing **"The Tyler 4" ™Fundamentals™** to sell his HR program. . . .

Craig carefully prepared his Presentation/Demonstration™ on his computer. He gathered information about the current need for management training, evaluated the effectiveness of the program he was proposing and even included testimonials from other companies that had implemented this program. He tailored his Presentation/Demonstration™ to each department head, putting in each department's unique numbers and including testimonials from people in similar areas of other companies.

**Commit your Presentation/Demonsration™
to memory.**

Next, Craig set up formal meetings with each department head. He was dressed professionally and was ready to leverage the rapport he'd developed over the previous few months. With John, the head of field operations, Craig told a story of a time when he was working in the field and how difficult it had been to get a response from HR in the corporate office. He quickly added that this was why he makes sure that all HR employees understand that the company's employees are HR's *"customers."*

"Craig, I had no idea you once worked in field operations." John said in a very surprised voice.

"Oh yes, for six years," Craig responded. "That's why this new program is so important to me; I know what a difference it can make in the lives of your people!"

John was impressed with the Presentation/Demonstration™ and told Craig that this was an excellent program. He could see now how it would improve the leadership skills of the field managers while reducing turnover costs. This would lead to increased productivity and more profits!

But Craig didn't stop there; he went for the agreement!

Craig: "John, based on what we've discussed, don't you think that this HR program would make your life and the lives of your employees better?"

John: "Yes, Craig, I do!"

Craig: "And you see how this program will save your area a great deal of money and will increase your sales as well?"

John: "Yes, your presentation proved that to me."

Craig: "Let's fill out this budget request paperwork and approve it together. I am excited about putting our new plan into action as soon as possible. It is never too soon to start making the company more money, wouldn't you agree?"

John: "I do agree. Where do I put my autograph?"

That year at budget time, every department head was committed to seeing this new program implemented. Craig received the resources he needed to have a successful and effective HR management training program. . . .

In our example, Craig's **Commitment to *EXCELLENCE*™** paid off—not just for him, but for the whole company. The moral of this story is simple: To achieve excellence as an HR professional, you must clearly understand your sales role.

I leave you with two thoughts. First, to be a masterful HR professional you *must* understand and master sales, so enroll in a sales education program and reap the rewards. Second, **"Remember that your success tomorrow is in direct proportion to your Commitment to *EXCELLENCE*™ today."**™

About The Author

Richard Tyler

Richard Tyler is the CEO of **Richard Tyler International, Inc.™** an organization named one of the top training and consulting firms in the world. Mr. Tyler's success in sales, quality improvement, management and customer service and his reputation for powerful educational methods and motivational techniques, has made him one of the most sought after consultants, lecturers and teachers. Mr. Tyler shares his philosophies with millions of individuals each year through keynote speaking, syndicated writing, radio, television, seminars, books and tapes. Mr. Tyler's book "*SMART BUSINESS STRATEGIES*™, *The* **Guide to Small Business Marketing** *EXCELLENCE*" has been hailed as one of the best books ever written for small-business marketing. His philosophies have been featured in *Entrepreneur Magazine*® as well as in hundreds of articles and interviews. Mr. Tyler is the founder of the **LEADERSHIP FOR TOMORROW™** an organization dedicated to educating young adults in the importance of **self-esteem, goal setting** and **lifelong success.** He also serves as a board member to such community organizations as **Be an Angel Fund**, a non-profit organization helping multiple handicapped children to have a better life.

Richard Tyler International, Inc.™
P.O. BOX 630249
Houston, TX 77263-0249
phone: 713-974-7214
email: RichardTyler@RichardTyler.com
website: http://www.RichardTyler.com
website: http://www.TylerTraining.com
website: http://www.ExcellenceEdge.com

Chapter Ten

Human Resource Development Around The Globe

Donna Steffey, MBA

Three-year-old Liu Xiao had never seen a foreigner up close. On February 5, 2003, a tall, blonde, blue-eyed stranger greeted her as she arrived home from preschool. With my limited Chinese vocabulary, I said, "Ni Hao, Wa ei ni" as we met. My "Hello, I love you" was welcomed by the only English Liu Xiao knew. With shrieks and laughter, she ran around the room shouting, "Happy Birthday to you!" Experiencing Chinese culture firsthand and developing "guanxi" (the Chinese word for "relationships") was an unexpected and wonderful benefit of my business trip to China, where I had gone to deliver a train-the-trainer course in human resource development.

Globalization is a leading and constant topic of discussion amongst many HRD professionals. Yet some feel it may never have an impact on them. Where you fall on the "globalization continuum" may depend on the organization you are with, how familiar you are with globally diverse business cultures, how well you can adapt to the global marketplace and how well you are able to conduct training and development with international business partners.

But whether you work as part of an international organization or as an independent consultant, you will probably soon be dealing with global issues. In the emerging borderless economy, cultural barriers are presenting both new challenges and new opportunities for HRD professionals. The marketplace is becoming increasingly diverse, and business is undergoing a major transformation. As these changes occur, we need cultural as well as business information to prepare our corporate partners and ourselves for the journey ahead. According to *Training and Development* magazine, culturally competent leadership development is the number one global HR priority, followed by the ability to develop, recruit and retain outstanding talent around the world.[1]

In the emerging borderless economy, cultural barriers are presenting both new challenges and new opportunities for HRD professionals.

As HRD specialists, our calling is becoming broader than human resource development. We have an opportunity to create collaborative relationships to foster international understanding and respect in a multicultural world. While national governments have the primary responsibility for maintaining peace, they are limited in what they can actually do to ensure a peaceful world. Individuals and organizations can make tremendous contributions through their actions abroad. I was training in China on September 11, 2001. I saw firsthand how a practitioner could make a global difference. Many of my participants had never met an American before our training. When the buildings fell, we cried together. They saw our grief. They had gotten to know our training team and could put a face on the buildings that had fallen thousands of miles away.

This chapter is about learning to think and act in culturally respectful ways. It offers you a starting point in your quest for knowledge about international HRD best practices and challenges. You will learn about regional and global trends affecting international business development and, therefore, human resource development. You will find information about global trends in workplace learning and performance based on benchmarking studies done in ten regions of the world during the past four years. You will read about cultural differences and suggestions on how to prepare yourself

---

[1] Rich Willins and Sheila Rioux. The Growing Pains of Globalizing HR, Training and Development Magazine, May 2000

for business abroad—including how to avoid being "The Ugly American." Finally, you will get a brief overview of seven global regions, their national challenges, cultural differences and HR practices. So grab your suitcase and your passport and let's start our journey.

Global Business Trends

Globalization is defined as "a universal flow of goods, information and services across political, financial, technical and cultural boundaries."[2] Over the past decade, there has been a far-reaching move toward capitalism and consumerism around the globe. With the proliferation and convenience of modern technology and the systematic erosion of trade barriers, many companies have developed a global presence—in spite of a slowdown in the U.S. and world economies.

Some U.S. corporations have turned to cheap labor in developing countries to keep prices and expenses in line. As a result, a tsunami of U.S. jobs has swept onto foreign shores. While the U.S. has tried to discourage companies from outsourcing to lower-cost locales such as China and India, the economics of "offshoring" may just be too powerful for business to resist. Human resource departments will have to be able to manage a more cross-cultural, diverse and foreign workforce as this trend continues.

One challenge of globalization is waiting for the building of infrastructures, including electricity, roads and phone lines in developing countries. Beyond this, it is likely that sporadic backlashes against globalization, language barriers, high illiteracy rates and clashing social norms will present even greater challenges.

According to researchers (Rosen et. al., 2000), other trends that will present challenges during this new stage of business include:

- European Integration - The economic integration of Europe and the euro will solidify that continent's influence over the world stage.

- American Backlash - Defensiveness against American culture, democracy, military might and free-market capitalism will undermine the continuing strength of the U.S.

- Asian Rebound - The hardworking nature of Asians and their social and family ties, combined with their commitment to education, form a strong impetus for their economies to rebound.

---

[2] Bierema, Laura. The Global Pendulum, TD, 2002

- China, Inc. - If China continues on its current path, it will become the largest, most important market in the world.

- Ethnic Conflicts - The number and intensity of ethnic conflicts will increase and continue worldwide as terrorism continues.

- Economics Versus Environmentalism - As economic development expands globally, pollution, deforestation and global warming will hasten, causing more political conflicts.

- Generational Demographics - The swelling population of young people in the developing countries and the need to educate and create jobs for them, combined with the growth of the elderly population and the need to take care of them, will create economic and political challenges for all.[3]

Given all these challenges, the role of human resource development must change. We will need to build and develop the capabilities of the organization to thrive amidst these global issues rather than simply reacting to more traditional issues such as performance management, class size and blended learning approaches—and we have to do it in a culturally responsive way. An HR system that is common practice in your country may be considered offensive in another. Differences in employment laws, compensation packages, job security and learning styles are just a few examples of what an HR professional might face working globally versus locally.

Learning and teaching styles differ among cultures as well as individuals. For example, the entertaining instructional style of the U.S. facilitator does not find a receptive audience in many corners of the globe. A few years ago, I spent some time facilitating programs in the UK. The evaluations had a consistent message: "Too American." How could it be? I had changed all my business examples! It took me about a week to realize that it was my style and not my content that was "too American." By easing the British audience into my entertaining style rather than overwhelming them with it, they reacted more like frogs put into cool water instead of boiling water. They were able to bathe in the knowledge, as opposed to hopping out of the classroom, overwhelmed by my "Americanism."

---

[3] Enter the Brave New World: Trends Affecting International Business Development, Workforce Management, 2003, www.workforce.com
Global Literacies:Lessons on Business Leadership and National Culture, Robert Rosen, Particia Dign, Marshall Singer, and Carl Phillips (Simon & Schuster, 2000)

The bottom line for global companies—no matter where they're based—is the need for the development of globally literate leadership. New educational strategies are needed to cultivate global leaders. By helping leaders build core competencies for success in the global marketplace, we will become indispensable to businesses and surely give them the return on investment of training dollars that organizations are looking for.

Trends in Workplace Learning and Performance

Organizations and workers need to cope with changes, create new tactics for prolonged corporate success and increase knowledge and skills to compete in a global environment. Given these needs, is it any wonder that workplace learning has grown in importance?

Since 1997, the American Society for Training and Development (ASTD), an international association of performance-improvement specialists, has been collecting benchmarking data to measure and compare worldwide patterns in workplace learning.[4] ASTD's latest State of the Industry Report, compiled by Brenda Sugrue, was published in December 2003. Two hundred seventy-six U.S. companies and 192 non-U.S. companies, representing ten different regions of the world, shared their data. The companies included agricultural, manufacturing, transportation and finance/insurance organizations. The measurement kit focused on a common set of definitions and metrics. Note that the report is based on a sample of organizations that, by participating, have demonstrated a strong interest in HRD. There is no way for ASTD to know how closely these samples represent training practices within each region.

U.S. Trends

- Training hours per employee have increased since 2001.
- Delivery via learning technologies increased in all study organizations in 2002. It is expected to have increased in 2003 as well. This trend helps organizations train across multiple locations locally and globally.

---

[4] Surgue, Brenda. State of the Industry, American Society for Training and Development, 2003, www.ASTD.org

- The employee groups receiving the largest percentage of training expenditures were customer service and production employees.

- There was a big decline in the percentage of expenditures that went to training executives and senior managers.

- The percentage of training delivered via classrooms is projected to continue its decrease to below sixty-five percent of training delivered.

International Comparisons

- Organizations in Africa and Australia/New Zealand have consistently trained the highest percentage of eligible employees (ninety percent in 2002). Japanese and Latin American organizations consistently trained the lowest percentage (around sixty percent). U.S. organizations trained an average of seventy-nine percent of employees.

- In 2002, Japanese organizations were the biggest users of learning technologies, delivering twenty percent of training via technology compared to fifteen percent in U.S. organizations. Organizations in Latin America delivered the smallest percentage of training via technology, at around three percent.

- When converted to U.S. dollars, organizations in Middle Eastern countries, Australia/New Zealand and the U.S. consistently spent the most dollars per employee, while African and Latin American organizations consistently spent the fewest.

- Mentoring and coaching programs were used by seventy-five percent or more of the firms in all regions, except for the U.S., where sixty-nine percent of the organizations employed this practice.

Other HRD practices that were measured in this study included job rotation, use of task forces, employee access to key business information, employee involvement in business decisions, total quality management (TQM) and self-directed work teams. Fifty percent or more of responding organizations across all regions reported using all six of these HRD practices.[5]

- TQM was used most frequently in the Middle East, where ninety-two percent of respondents reported its use; it was used least in Latin American organizations, where seventy percent of organizations reported using it.

- The most popular compensation practice used was incentive compensation. Australia/New Zealand organizations use knowledge- or skill-based pay. This was also heavily used in Asia.

- Use of annual performance reviews was almost universal. The only two regions that did not report 100-percent usage were the U.S. and Europe. The use of peer review varied by region and was least used in Chinese organizations.

Now that you have had a brief overview of global HRD trends, let's talk about cultural differences and how they may affect you as an HR specialist.

Cultural Impact on HRD

"Culture is the collective programming of the mind which distinguishes the people of one category of people from another," says Geert Hofstede, a Dutch interculturalist. Each nation indoctrinates its members with a common array of behavioral norms that leads to sets of national behavioral characteristics. These characteristics permeate every aspect of life, including behavior in the workplace, and impact the way organizations do business.[6]

When we look at individualism vs. collectivism, for example, we know there is a difference between the East and the West.[7] During every stage of education and "programming" in the West (Europe, U.S., Canada), people learn to accept personal responsibility and view themselves primarily as individuals. Conversely, at every stage of personal development in the East (Japan, China, Singapore), people learn to see themselves as small parts of a larger society and emphasize the importance of group agreement and a consensus approach.

---

[5] The 2002 ASTD International Comparison Report, Alexandria, VA, American Society for Training and Development, 2002 www.astd.org

[6] Does Culture Matter?, Global Business Culture 2002, www.globalbusinessculture.com

[7] Sarkar-Barney, Shreya. The Role of National Culture in Enhancing Training Effectiveness: A Framework, 2003

Language often reflects cultural differences, even among nations that share a common language. When Donna Baylor of Transition Seminars taught in the UK, she referred to her purse as her "fanny pack." After a few days, someone finally informed her that she was using a dirty word. Cynthia Hernandez Kolski of Communication Education says that when she went to Mexico to teach stress management and communication skills, she had to be very careful with her communication. Even though she speaks Spanish, she realized that literal translations and conveying her intended meaning resulted in two very different messages.

Another important difference is how verbosely or concisely a particular culture speaks. In Italy, for example, the ability to speak well using a large volume of words is a sign of being intellectual. In other countries, however, being talkative is viewed differently, perhaps negatively; or it may even cause problems. Wei Xian Lin, my co-facilitator and translator while I was training in China, was interpreting a rather lengthy program for me. We were alarmed when we heard a loud thud. Not only had one of our participants fallen asleep but he had actually fallen off his chair. He was out cold! In this case, my verbosity caused a potentially serious problem!

Culture influences approaches to everyday situations in the work environment in hundreds of ways. National characteristics play an important role in determining corporate strategies, incentive programs, personnel policies and training strategies. It is dangerous to ignore these differences. Most organizations know they must invest the time and money to research government rules and regulations and regional market conditions, but in HRD, we sometimes make the mistake of thinking that "people are people" and will all learn effectively through the same learning materials as long as we change the examples. Or we may believe that we can use the same incentive programs overseas that work in the U.S. In order to minimize the potential risks of working internationally, it is important to look first at the people and their culture to understand what drives and motivates them.

Before looking at specific regional characteristics, though, let's check ourselves and be sure that we are culturally and socially literate—seeing, thinking and acting in culturally mindful ways.

Get Ready to Go Global

Bags all packed, briefcase and passport in hand, we're ready to go. But are you aware of the "cultural" items in your suitcase that you are about to subconsciously communicate to your unsuspecting global partner? Chances are you don't. Our culture is the paradigm through which we see the world, and unless we are conscious of it, we probably won't be able to really see and learn about the culture we are about to experience. For instance, what are some of our collective attitudes that sometimes cause locals to label us "Ugly Americans"?

1. Americans believe in having control over their environment. Problems in one's life (such as poverty), they conclude, are due to laziness and an unwillingness to take responsibility and work harder. This can create an attitude of superiority.

2. Americans see change as good, leading to development and progress. Many older, more traditional cultures see change as disruptive to their ancient heritage. This American attitude can manifest itself as disrespect.

3. Americans are more concerned about getting things accomplished on time than about developing interpersonal relationships.

4. Equality is cherished in the U.S. The concept of equality is strange to seven eighths of the world, which view status and authority as desirable.

5. Competition is the "American Way." Americans believe it brings out the best in any individual.

6. Informal and casual attitudes permeate every aspect of American life. Bosses even encourage workers to use first names.

7. Many other countries have developed subtle, sometimes highly ritualistic ways of informing others of unpleasant information. Americans prefer the direct approach.

Having said all this, Tom West of The Soliv (Soliv) Group, LLC found it necessary to be a bit of an "Ugly American" just once. Tom and five colleagues traveled to Copenhagen, Denmark, to become certified in a program that they would later introduce into the United States. A major difference between a Danish two-week training program and its American counterpart is that the Danes train well into the night, with a break for dinner. Then they often party for the rest of the evening as a "bonding experience." The Danes did not realize that this was not part of the American business culture but assumed that with the "relaxed" American attitude that it would be appreciated. The American group could only do this for four days. On the fifth day, the tired group got "ugly" and revolted. "We're spent!" they bellowed. "We can't think anymore!" The Danes quickly realized the faux pas and gave the Americans the rest of the afternoon off for sightseeing.

It is easy to get overwhelmed when you think of all the ways you must prepare yourself to go global. Tucker International, a full-service, international HRD company, advises us to gather as much information about current events in that country as possible.[8] We also need an understanding of any tensions that exist between our host country and home country. Not only must cultural differences be understood socially but also differences in business practices, laws and governmental policies.

Culture shock is to be expected, and an adaptation period is normal. A few additional points:

- Travel in a spirit of humility with a genuine desire to learn more about the people of your host country. In each country where I have taught, I found that sitting down to a family meal with local people gave me a great insight into the true culture of the area.

- Different cultures hold different concepts of time. Learn to respect the time concepts of people in your host culture.

- Acquaint yourself with local customs. I remember fumbling with my chopsticks at a business luncheon in Asia. My host removed them from the table and replaced them all with forks. I had to watch uncomfortably as my new colleagues soberly struggled with forks for the rest of the meal. Added to that, I had chosen a soft drink when it was customary to order the local wine.

- Working with a translator can be difficult. Even if the translator understands English, he or she may not understand the nuances necessary for business communication. Be prepared to re-explain a concept many different ways.

- Put aside any preconceived notions and biases about the "American" way of doing things.

- Research, research, research. Barry Pilkington, while working for Motorola, was sent to Japan to deliver a series of half-day training sessions to the Japanese sales reps there. He was informed that everyone would be housed at a traditional Japanese resort, but he did not research his

---

[8] Best Practices Make for Perfect International Assignments, Tucker International Press Articles, 2001, www.tucherintl.com

accommodations. He was very surprised when the group wanted to cut the meeting short midday to take baths. He soon realized that they were referring to the traditional baths fed by the resort's hot springs. Barry was even more surprised when the hotel began to distribute room keys and he found out that there would be six people to a room with a traditional Japanese style toilet! Research, research, research!

Region-Specific Data

This section serves as a brief overview of seven globally diverse regions around the world. It is designed to increase your cultural awareness, but it is not extensive enough to prepare you to do business in other countries. Prior to any overseas assignment, I recommend that you do thorough research on any organization you will be working with, just as you would in the US. Then do additional research on the host country and its culture. Read books (including novels) to learn about their modern and ancient history and culture, view foreign films, talk to people who have lived in the country and ask them to compare the two cultures, read the local newspaper online, and try to learn some of the language or expressions. People you meet will appreciate your effort.

Here are the seven regions at a glance with more expansive data to follow.

Country	Size of Labor Force (thousand)	Unemployment Rate	Population Growth Rate %	Literacy Rate %
Canada	16,400	7.2	0.96	97
China	706,000	10	0.87	81.5
Mid East	15,333	11.3	1.98	76
Europe	11,103	6.45	0.28	98.5
India	406,000	4.4	1.51	52
Japan	67,700	4.9	0.15	99
South Africa	17,000	37	0.02	85
United States	141,800	6	0.89	97

Data Source: CIA World Factbook[9]

---

[9] GlobalEDGE Country Comparison Feature, wwwlglobaledge.msu.edu

Canada Can Do

A wide assortment of circumstances challenges the Canadian economy today, including geopolitical tensions, continued sluggishness of the U.S. economy and the 2003 impact of SARS. Despite these factors—and a softer labor market—signs of a healthy economy are appearing. Along with economic recovery will come a growing need for human resource development. The increased employment of knowledge workers and the growing number of Canadian employers who report having difficulty recruiting qualified employees raise questions about what Canada is doing to respond to an apparent employee shortage. It is said that in 2004, seventy percent of new jobs will require a post-secondary education—a university degree will be required for twenty-five percent of these. According to the ASTD State of the Industry Report, seventy-nine percent of employees receive training. Some organizations are looking into "variable pay plans," which tie a portion of an employee's income to performance as a means of attracting and retaining qualified candidates. Hewitt, a global human resource outsourcing and consulting firm, surveyed 345 Canadian companies nationwide and found that average salary increases for 2004 are projected to be 3.3 percent overall, which is expected to outpace the inflation rate.[10]

The average age in Canada reached an historical peak in 2001, when it stood at 37.6 years. The aging population means that HR managers are now called upon to provide effective succession planning at a time when fewer and fewer young people live there. Another demographic prediction indicates that by 2011, the net growth of Canada's population will be entirely related to immigration. HR must be prepared to manage the integration of cultures and diversity in the workplace.

---

[10] Hewitt Study Shows Canadian Companies Hold the Line for 2003 Salary Budgeting, 2003, www.hewitt.com

Made in China

By Wei Xiao Lin
Xian, China

China's entry into the World Trade Organization has brought its labor force unprecedented business and job opportunities. The Chinese government is starting to prepare its workforce to be white-collar professionals. Yet Chinese enterprises did not pay much attention to human resource development until the country carried out "reform and opening up" policies around 1980. The first reform was the era of the agricultural economy, when land was the most valuable resource. Next came the industrial economy , in which capital or money was the most valuable resource; it was necessary for equipment, real estate, and stock purchases. Now under the information economy, the importance of human resources development has become obvious, especially since high-caliber employees are increasingly pulled away from local enterprises by foreign firms. These foreign firms offer salaries that are ten to twenty times higher than Chinese firms can offer. On many public occasions, President Jiang Zemin has emphasized, "Human resources are the most valuable resources in China." China's leaders have had to reconsider their HR arrangements, which in the past tightly controlled labor force mobility.

While Chinese enterprises are experiencing increasingly severe competition for talent from foreign companies, training—which is still done only on a small scale there—is usually available only to senior managers and is regarded more as a perk than a targeted training effort. Only in the past couple of years have attitudes toward training begun to change. Previously, enterprises did not think they had the responsibility to train employees, whom they felt should be qualified enough to meet job requirements. They felt it was the duty of employees to train themselves. Some ancient cultural wisdom also holds back training efforts. There is a Chinese saying that goes: "There is no capable soldier under the leadership of a smart general." Another saying that many believe is: "Birds that sing are very likely to be shot." Managers did not want employees who were smarter than they were, and employees knew to pretend not to be smarter than their bosses.

Although training efforts in China have increased, they are still applied unsystematically. Most companies don't have training-development plans and will accept any random training available.

There is little knowledge about how to distinguish the good from the bad or the ugly. According to the ASTD State of the Industry Report, only 5.9 percent of training is done via learning technologies. In addition, most classroom training is strictly lecturing, with little participant interaction. Methods of delivery are changing, but the cost of training technology remains prohibitive for most enterprises. A large number of low-skilled workers must be retrained or let go from the increasingly competitive marketplace. The "Iron-rice bowl" is no longer iron, and workers over age forty are finding it difficult to find or keep jobs.

India Rising

The global market growth in India has only been strong in the last decade, even though India has always had brilliant, educated people. I once co-facilitated a leadership-training course for Infosys Technologies, one of India's largest software companies and an outstanding learning organization. A student asked his fellow participants to "raise their hands if they had been the top student in their university class." Every hand in the room went up. According to *BusinessWeek*, "If India can turn into a fast-growth economy, it will be the first developing nation that used its brainpower, not natural resources or raw muscle of factory labor, as the catalyst."[11]

It wasn't until July 1991 that radical economic liberalization measures were launched. Between 1947 and 1991, there was a protected market with strict foreign exchange regulations and lengthy licensing procedures. Then the IT boom occurred in 2000. India now possess some basic underpinnings of a strong, market-driven economy: democratic government, Western accounting principals and the widespread use of English.

Still, this country—with its abundance of low-cost, high-IQ, English-speaking brainpower—has its challenges. Only fifty-two percent of India's billion-person population is literate, and only slightly more than that have electricity in their homes. Tensions between Hindus and Muslims are problematic, and the risk of war with nuclear-armed Pakistan is ever present.

Training and development have grown rapidly in India. Spending on training has tripled in four years. The percentage of employees receiving training has jumped from less than half to nearly two

---

[11] The Rise of India, BusinessWeek online, 2003,
www.businessweek.com/magazine/content/03_49/b3861001_mz001.htm

thirds. Since much of India's business involves Western partners, they feel a strong need to incorporate Western concepts, models and theories. Don Overbey of SunCatcher Productions recently consulted with a company in Mumbai, India. The Indians wanted to operate their new marketing division like the Americans do, so they contracted with Don to recommend a "world-class" Western structure. They adopted his company's recommendations, but Don was concerned about the cultural differences. The Indians, however, have become proficient at adapting American concepts to fit their culture. That is how they have become so competitive globally.

As a whole, the Indian economy today is following the pattern set by its Western counterparts. The software, telecom and manufacturing industries are feeling the impact of the mild recession. Restructuring and downsizing are the main concerns of the HRD professionals there. Indian organizations see the need to support training efforts and human resource development in order to attract and retain qualified candidates.

Japan's Workforce Becomes More Fluid

As Japan's workforce moves from the concept of "lifetime employment" to a more fluid model along international standards, changing jobs in Japan is no longer rare. This is good news for the foreign associate interested in hiring talented, experienced workers. There will still be some challenges, however, since the Japanese view Western business in a negative light. Japanese see a greater likelihood of dismissals from Western companies—compared to Japanese companies—due to an about-face from leaders in offshore international headquarters.

Japan's economy roared in the 1980s, but the country has faced a slowdown since the 1990s. Despite its current problems, Japan still possesses the fundamentals for strong economic recovery and growth. It has great manufacturing capacity, advanced technology, heavy investment in education—with 72.5 percent of its workforce having attended universities—and a disciplined workforce.[12]

Japan's strong cultural influences affect its workforce. The emphasis placed on seniority in the workplace is a unique characteristic of the Japanese labor market. It is no surprise that younger workers are opposing that tradition in favor of performance promotions.

---

[12] Gross, Ames, Trends in Human Resources Practices in Japan. SHRM International Focus, 1998, www.pacificbridge.com

Changing the seniority system can help organizations, because younger workers may then be more willing to speak up without the fear of appearing disrespectful. Younger workers can bring their knowledge of communication technology and global business practices to the discussion table. There is also a strong tradition of group consensus that affects corporate decision making. The advantage of involving employees from all levels of an organization in the decision-making process is that it is easier to implement new ideas, even if they take longer to decide upon.

Although lifetime employment had many negative effects, it did provide Japanese companies with workforce security. Guaranteed employment and a secure salary have traditionally promoted employee loyalty. Companies poured significant investments into employee training, feeling secure that employees would stay.

Japan has a 95-to-1 ratio of employees per training staff member. Twenty percent of their training is done via learning technology, and sixty-five percent is done via classroom training. The low ratio of trainers to learners may help to explain a cultural difference in learning styles. The Japanese have a very relaxed learning style. Julie Jacques, director of training and development for a company in Schaumburg, Illinois, recalls the time she was facilitating product and sales training for a group in Tokyo. She says she was quite humbled by the fact that many participants had their eyes closed. Nothing feels worse for a trainer than being perceived as so boring that people are sleeping through her training program! She was relieved when, after class, someone told her that it was quite common for participants to close their eyes. Julie says, "Perhaps it wasn't my training after all!"

Africa and the Middle East

Africa and the Middle East regions, except for the oil-rich countries, will have to create five to six million jobs each year if current unemployment is to be reduced. Recent downward trends in birth rates have not significantly impacted the labor force yet. Unemployment is running between twenty and thirty percent. The public sector and the informal economy continue to account for most jobs. At least twenty percent of the total population in this area are between ages fifteen and twenty-four, and unemployment has affected youth more than others.[13]

---

[13] Labor Market and Human Resource Development, Economic Research Forum, 2001

Female workers in the region concentrate in a small number of economic activities, are less mobile and face barriers in many professions. The good news is that current market reforms are creating more jobs for women.

Too many training programs in the region produce poor results. Often funded from payroll contributions, they are costly, supply driven and dominated by governments. They often serve as programs of last resort for educational dropouts. These training programs lack facilities and equipment and are not sufficiently geared to the needs of the market.

Fortunately, things are improving. Nancy Kramer, director of business and industry services at Harold Washington College in Chicago, knows this firsthand. Nancy decided to foster collaborative relationships and international understanding and increase her cultural mindfulness by becoming a Peace Corps volunteer in Zimbabwe. She made a difference in the way training was delivered when she taught "How to Start a Small Business." When she arrived in Masvingo, she found that local Zimbabwe entrepreneurs wanted to learn everything the American way. But as Nancy began to understand the culture, she realized that American ways were not the best ways in Zimbabwe. She taught the curriculum and invited the local business owners to be guest speakers so they could expand on the reality and application of ideas in Zimbabwe. She utilized role-playing in her classes as well. Once the students learned it, they loved it. Nancy said, "Everyone was a ham. They especially loved pretending to be the manager." Nancy says that this experience helped her to learn to laugh a lot, especially at herself!

The oil-rich countries in the area paint a different training picture. It appears that organizations in these Middle Eastern countries spend more than any other organizations in the world on training—averaging $989 per employee, training eighty-two percent of their employees and utilizing learning technologies 9.4 percent of the time.

South Africa—Rich in Resources

South Africa has the most sophisticated free-market economy on the African continent. The country accounts for only three percent of the continent's land mass but generates twenty-five percent of its gross domestic product. Like other developing countries, South Africa has a flourishing international business community operating alongside a large, subsistent, informal business sector. It is experiencing an inflation rate of about ten percent.

South Africa is rich in natural resources yet has a shortage of skilled labor and local capital. Apartheid South Africa spent a disproportionate amount of resources equipping a small section of society, mainly whites. As a result, the country now faces a shortage of skilled labor. This is compounded by what some call a "brain drain" and what others call the "white flight." According to a South African labor market study, emigration is highest in education, engineering and medicine. The economy is characterized by a racially biased distribution of wealth and skills. Unemployment is at around thirty percent.[14]

What is South Africa doing to retain its skilled labor? Lebogang Lombard, senior HR development manager at diamond company De Beers, says, "We pay people well and invest unashamedly in their development. We also rotate them internationally so they will bring their global experience back."[15] The government is reviewing the immigration laws to attract skilled labor with expertise. The government has also made a decision to make HIV drug treatments available to pregnant women. Organizations are faced with increasing pressure on retirement funds and medical aid due to a preponderance of AIDS-related deaths.

While ninety percent of eligible employees at South African companies are being trained, expenditures for training—$138 per employee—are lower than those for any other group in the international comparison study done by ASTD.

Europe Unites

The European Union today faces many important issues. The Charter for Fundamental Rights will decide to what extent the EU should attempt to act as one decision-making body on important human rights issues. They will evaluate the right to collective bargaining, the right to fair and just working conditions and the links between productivity and living standards. There is pressure to further deregulate economies in major EU member states, such as France and Germany, to alleviate high unemployment there. Many of the countries want various aspects of the Anti-Discrimination Directive enforced, such as prohibiting discrimination on the grounds of sexual orientation, religion, disabilities or age.

Another area of serious concern is labor costs. Costs vary greatly throughout the EU; they were highest in Denmark and Germany and

---

[14] Tsukudu, Tiisetso. Brain Drain or Gain. Worldlink, CIPD/PPL, 2002
[15] IPM South Africa Regional Report, Worldlink, CIPD/PPL, 2002

lowest in Portugal and Sweden. See www.europe.eu.int for current figures.[16]

The workplace in Europe is facing some major changes. Workforce diversity is increasing, and employee competence is considered to be of primary importance. Learning technologies in Europe account for 7.6 percent of training delivery. Although it makes sense to use this delivery method to train such a wide geographic area, the disparity between the amount of usage in Europe and the U.S. reflects both technology and cultural differences. "The individualistic culture in the U.S. brings an assumption that workplace learners are motivated to learn in order to improve their performance. The collectivist culture of many European countries supports the idea of learning as a social process," says Jane Massy, a European e-learning expert. Internet access and usage are also lower in Europe than in the U.S., and Europeans have a greater variance of information networks. Multiple language barriers compound their problems.

Where Do We Go Next?

Human resource development experts have a challenging job, given the realities of the U.S. and the global marketplace. Healthcare costs are soaring, workplaces are becoming increasingly diverse culturally, and profits are sagging. Baby Boomers everywhere are aging, and there aren't enough young skilled workers to plug into the labor force. ASTD reports that organizations with above-average training and development budgets outperform competitors and achieve a higher total shareholder return. Many of the top firms clearly understand this concept. Our skills are needed and our industry future looks bright.

Our HRD challenge, then, is to build world-class organizations by designing training strategies that augment participants' knowledge about their businesses, cultivate current global leaders and develop new ones, and help companies identify and build the core competencies necessary to excel in the global marketplace. We can continue to use the HRD tools and techniques that have gotten us this far but our focus must be on our end goal and not just on the process to get there. And what is the end goal for HRD professionals? Is a goal of "helping to build world-class organizations" enough? Peter Block, respected author and humanist said in a recent T&D article, "If an organization

---

[16] EAPM Regional Report, World Federation of Personnel Management Association: Worldlink, 2003

exists to be efficient and customer focused it that compelling enough to retain and motivate employees? Organizations that have a compelling purpose matter most to employees."[17] So our challenge may go even deeper. As HRD professionals we possess certain insights and intuitions about people due to our access and observation of employees and management. Maybe our challenge is to push the boundaries and help shape management's thinking. We have the power to use our understanding of basic cross cultural human behavior to influence organizations to identify and achieve more than being a world-class organization. With our influence they can be a compelling positive "world-class" force.

---

[17] The Future of the Profession formerly known as Training, T&D, Dec 2003 Pat Galagan

About The Author

Donna Steffey

Donna Steffey, MBA, is an energizing consultant, author, radio personality and sought after speaker who has helped improve performance and output on four continents. Global organizations in the US, UK, Australia and China have found participants were more productive, leadership driven and culturally mindful of their communication approach after attending her programs. She is President of Vital Signs, an international training and development firm that Vitalizes People, Performance and Profits with award winning programs in a variety of industries. Donna is currently president of the Chicago Chapter of the American Society for Training and Development. The Chicago Chapter is a recognized leading chapter because of its award winning publications, Train-the-Trainer programs which Donna taught in China, and the fact that it is the largest chapter in the world with over 1200 training and organization development experts. You know Donna is a great communicator and leader since she has been chosen to lead her peers in becoming more influential locally and globally. Donna is part of an outstanding faculty team at Lake Forest Graduate School of Management Corporate Education in Lake Forest, IL. They won the 2001 ASTD Excellence in Practice Award for Managing Change. ASTD states, "This award recognizes and celebrates outstanding contributions and achievements in advancing learning and performance in the workplace. The work of the individuals, teams, and organizations being honored illustrates the impact learning and performance has on creating a competitive advantage for business and organizations worldwide." Donna is a member of the National Speakers Association, International Association of Human Resource Information Management, and winner of the Speaking Professional Award from NSA Illinois.

Donna Steffey, MBA
Vital Signs
40 Delburne
Davis, IL. 61019
Tel: (815) 248-3104
Fax: (847) 991-0217
Email: itrainum@starband.net
www.Vitalsignstraining.com

Chapter Eleven

Turning Managers Into Leaders

Sylvia Henderson, MBA

**Leadership and learning are indispensable to
each other.**

*– John F. Kennedy, 35th President of the
United States of America*

Human Resources.

Are the people in your business or organization important to you?
If they are–and they had better be if you want your business to succeed–then your people resources, your human resources, must be
recognized, rewarded, acknowledged, promoted, trained and appreciated. People issues are human resource issues. If you are a business
owner, manager, supervisor or decision maker in an organization or
for your own business, then you have HR responsibilities and deal
with HR issues. Motivating your people and giving them the tools and
training to succeed are imperative to your long-term investment in
your human capital.

At some point in time you will identify and select people to move
into management and supervisory roles, whether as formal job titles
or by nature of their responsibilities. Quite often these people are

your top employees or most skilled trades people, technicians or professionals. They prove themselves excellent in their areas of expertise and by doing so, come to your attention as those who are eligible for greater responsibility. They become resources for others and are people to whom you can delegate some of the business operations and decision-making responsibilities that keep your business or organization running. How do you prepare these people to succeed as managers and leaders?

- Manager → a person who manages; esp. one who manages a business, institution, etc.
- Supervisor → a person who supervises (oversees, directs or manages workers, work, a project, etc.); manager; director.
- Leader → a person that leads; directing, commanding or guiding head, as of a group or activity.

— *Webster's New World Dictionary of the American Language.* *William Collins + World Publishing Co., Inc.*

On Becoming a New Manager

When I first was promoted to a management position where I was responsible for other people who directly reported to me, it was after having been a team and project leader for several years. My expertise as an employee was in the IT and training arenas. When I was promoted to a team and project leader, I had to step away from the day-to-day, hands-on technical and training tasks. I learned to focus on motivating people to work together toward shared business goals, planning and implementing schedules and processes, communicating with people throughout the organizational chain of command (people who had a wide range of communication skills themselves), making business presentations and providing the support–either through my own knowledge and skills or by acquiring other resources–needed to succeed. I had to lead without having the "power and authority" of being a manager with direct influence on employees' performance plans and compensation. Leaders I respected, both management and non-management, mentored and guided me through the process of moving from friend and co-worker to a respected leader and achiever of business objectives through other people.

My promotion to a management position where I had direct responsibility for the careers of the people in my department required my learning the organization's formal HR policies and procedures and meeting the management team expectations of the business. Fortunately, I just had to continue honing my leadership skills rather than learning to develop them upon promotion. Some of my management colleagues were not so fortunate.

All too often, I witnessed great employees getting promoted to managers and supervisors and experiencing difficulty in becoming respected leaders in their respective business areas and beyond. Many did not learn, or took a long time to learn, that managers and leaders are not one and the same.

Ken Blanchard, leadership guru and author of *Servant Leader, Leadership and the One-Minute Manager* and *Gung Ho!* (among numerous other books on leadership, management and customer service) notes that "The key to leadership today is influence, not authority." As a team and project leader, I had to learn the skills needed to influence people over whom I had little authority. The emphasis was on leading. As a manager, I had to learn the responsibilities of authority while incorporating the influencing skills to help the authority earn respect as a leader.

As a manager myself, I had to identify management candidates and prepare them for promotion to their new responsibilities. I questioned what characteristics and skills made a manager an effective leader and identified those I describe in this chapter. My research through the too-numerous-to-count volumes of management and leadership books, the hours spent attending seminars and training programs, and the successful experiences I encountered and facilitated in my career have repeatedly confirmed my observations and conclusions.

"Leadership, like management, is voluntary. You are not forced to hold your position. Leadership is also done best by example. Keeping that in mind – volunteer to lead by example – it will make all the difference in the workplace."

—Dennis Waitley, author of "The Winning Generation"

Your first step as a person responsible for moving people into supervisory positions is to identify the management candidate who exhibits some of the characteristics representative of an effective manager and strong leader.

When considering a person as a management candidate, step back and ask yourself the following questions to decide whether the candidate will likely make an effective manager–and leader.

What do you see in her?

☐ Is she a fantastic Web designer AND proactive in getting an entire Web design project completed on time and under budget?

☐ Does she produce high-quality widgets AND inspire her co-workers to increase the quality of theirs?

☐ Is the management candidate your top salesperson, or is she in the top ten percent AND maintaining strong relationships with her colleagues?

☐ Does the administrative employee support her manager or department effectively and efficiently as the "go-to" person AND take advantage of professional development opportunities, network beyond her area of responsibility and mentor others in her position to help them perform at their best?

☐ Is she a wonderful writer AND a great verbal and non-verbal communicator?

☐ Does she work hard, or does she work smart?

☐ Is she on the job twelve to fourteen hours per day, or does she have outside interests while still producing quality results on the job (work-life balance)?

☐ Does she focus on the minutiae of the next few days, or does she take into consideration the big picture and long term?

Good staff people, employees, professionals and skilled administrators can get things done.

- How well and how effectively do they get *others* to get things done?

- How much are they respected by others—both below and above them in rank and by their peers?

- Can they present information and ideas professionally and effectively and communicate with a wide range of people?

Being proactive when managing business functions. Meeting time and budget milestones. Inspiring and motivating others while garnering the respect of colleagues and management. Communicating effectively verbally, non-verbally and through the written word. Working smart. Maintaining a work-life balance. Influencing rather than commanding. These skills are representative of those used by a manager or supervisor who is a positive leader. If your management candidate needs to develop these skills, how do you go about helping him or her do so?

"There go my people. I must run to catch up with them for I am their leader."

— Ghandi (Mohandas K. Gandhi, Hindu crusader for passive resistance of injustice, 1869-1948)

Prepare Your New Manager/Supervisor for Success

When you promote someone to a management position, his success and effectiveness as a manager and leader is a reflection of your judgment in promoting that person and your ability to prepare him for his new responsibilities. You can choose any number or combination of actions to prepare your new manager for success:

- Mentor him yourself over an extended period of time.

- Send him to formal training at management training school—either internal to your organization or a contract or seminar company program.

- Hire a management coach for one-on-one coaching and development.

- Suggest media for his self-development–publications, audio, video and Web resources–providing management and leadership skills training.

- Teach by example. As you promote and manage other managers, you need to balance strategy and operations. Communicate top management's vision to those you manage and help them translate these strategic messages into operational activities.

- Provide a manager-in-training "apprenticeship" experience within your own or another organization.

- Encourage him to take advantage of professional development opportunities such as seminars, workshops, classes and conferences.

- Develop a leadership development action plan with the new manager and establish regular and open communications channels through which progress can be evaluated and guided.

Recognize your own strengths and weaknesses to decide if you have the skills to prepare and mentor the new manager through his transition. How do you rate yourself in:

- Feedback skills?
- Evaluation skills?
- Observation skills?
- Coaching skills?
- Your ability to be fair?
- Your ability to see the big picture?
- Your ability to get input from others (above, below and peers of the new manager)?

However you choose to prepare the management candidate for leadership, there are skills he should learn to enable him to succeed in his new position. These four competencies contribute a great deal to the success of the new manager or supervisor as an effective leader:

1. Basic leadership skills.

2. Staying technically current (in his areas of expertise) and maintaining positive relationships while considering the larger business picture and earning the respect of others.

3. Striking and encouraging a work-life balance in the midst of increasing demands.

4. Communicating effectively with employees, colleagues and upper management.

Sample Management Training Course Topics

This is a sample of the knowledge points and skills you should encourage your new supervisors to acquire:

- Listening skills.
- Management styles and the conditions under which each style is most appropriate.
- Strategic liaisons at all organizational levels.
- Organizational strategies and how to communicate them to the team → turning strategies into action plans.
- Critical success factors for achieving goals → their departments', teams', managements' and own goals.
- Values, priorities and work-life balance issues.
- Employee empowerment.
- Delegation skills.
- Giving and receiving feedback.
- Performance planning and evaluation.
- Managing change → organizational and personal.
- Coaching employees for performance and leadership.
- Working with a diverse workforce.
- Presentation skills.
- Problem-solving, decision-making and planning skills.
- Planning and running meetings.

> **"Leadership consists not in degrees of technique but in traits of character; it requires moral rather than athletic or intellectual effort, and it imposes on both leader and follower alike the burdens of self-restraint."**
>
> *— Lewis H. Lapham, Author of "Theatre of War"*

Manager to Leader: Leadership Skills

Up to this point I have been stating that a manager or supervisor is not a leader simply by her job title. There are specific characteristics of a leader that a manager must exhibit and practice in order to transcend her position of authority and be respected as a leader. Just what are these characteristics of an effective leader?

Dr. Charles Gordon, psychologist, author and founder of Gordon Training International, created the leadership model known as Leadership Effectiveness Training. His model is based on research that indicates that an effective leader must meet the organization's needs as a productivity specialist and meet the needs of her people and facilitate conflict resolution as a human relations specialist. Doing one without the other does not create an effective management/leadership balance.

Perform a search on the Internet for "leadership+characteristics" or read books and articles on being a leader and you will find a wide range of traits and behaviors identified as those of a leader. A repetitive pattern of characteristics appears throughout multiple sources, which I have used to create an acrostic that spells "LEADER".

A strong and effective leader characteristically:

L **Listens**. A leader is attentive to the needs and wants of her direct reports. She listens to what her people say verbally and what is communicated behind the words. Understanding what people need and want is essential to working with them to develop their knowledge and skills. A leader plays a large role in people development. Listening closely also reveals the pulse of the organization, which is important to the broader decision-making process affecting the success of the organization.

E **Effectively communicates** to people throughout all levels of the organization. From the time her promotion is announced, how the new manager communicates with people who report to her, her peer colleagues and those to whom she reports sets the tone for the remainder of her management experience. First impressions in her management role—even with people who are familiar with her as peers—set the stage for mutual respect, recognized authority and earned leadership.

A Is **action-oriented**. She is not afraid to get her hands dirty while simultaneously knowing when to avoid micromanaging the day-to-day operations of the business. She enables her subordinates and team members to grow and excel in their positions. She is able to set goals, lay the groundwork for achieving them and move people to action for accomplishing the goals.

D Is a **decision-maker**. She takes responsibility for situations within her control. She makes decisions rather than postpones them. She owns up to both the positives and the negatives of the results of her decisions. She solicits input from her team and uses what she learns to help in her decisions. She learns from her decisions and continues to make more.

E Is **easy to approach**. She is approachable and available to her people. Her door is open, and she maintains the confidences of those who approach her. She does not use information against others. She manages her time so that her availability does not overwhelm her own duties and interfere with achieving her own goals.

R **Relies on and influences other people**. She encourages teamwork to accomplish goals. She delegates ownership of tasks to others. She motivates others to achieve the goals of the organization as well as their own goals. She supports people's work-life balance so that they perform at their optimal levels of performance. She manages her human resources. She delegates to her people and empowers them to make decisions and take action while remaining responsible for the overall performance of her department.

Work with your new manager to help her learn or enhance these skills and acquire these characteristics. These leadership characteristics contribute to turning a person in a leadership position into a leader.

Luke: All right, I'll give it a try.
Yoda: No! Try not! Do or do not.
There is no try.

— *Yoda, to Luke Skywalker, Star Wars
Episode V: The Empire Strikes Back (1999)*

Backing Away Without Turning Off

Separating from old friendships and relationships and establishing new ones based on the new position of authority may be one of the most difficult processes for a new manager to go through if promoted from within the organization. Strong interpersonal relationships score high on the job satisfaction survey.

Job Satisfaction Survey – 2004: Summary Results

Top reasons for employee (management and non-management to-gether) job satisfaction:

- Communications between management and employees.
- Fair policies and procedures.
- Friends and relationships at work.
- Insurance benefits (cost and type).
- Job security.
- Pleasant physical working conditions and commute time.
- Recognition by management.
- Relationship with immediate supervisor.
- Salary/wages.

Job Satisfaction Survey 2004. E.A.Winning Associates.
www.ewin.com.

A new manager typically has a cadre of friends and colleagues with whom he carpools, takes breaks, goes to lunch, visits and other-wise commiserates throughout the business day. Some of these relationships transcend the professional environment into the per-sonal life of the supervisor. Past relationships built on being a skilled and respected employee must be severed–or at least distanced–in or-der to establish new relationships based on the management or supervisory position of authority. These new relationships must fre-quently be established with the very people the new manager once considered "untouchable" or "one of *them.*" This can create a feeling of being a turncoat or traitor to former colleagues and friends and may lead to a sense of isolation in the new position.

Help the new manager distance himself from those with whom he formerly was a co-worker. Distance will enable the new manager to more objectively handle personnel issues for the good of the organiza-tion–especially disciplinary and corrective actions. A manager needs the respect that distance can help more than friendships developed with direct reports. Distancing helps avoid appearances of favoritism. Distance does not mean superiority or aloofness or staying away from former peers. It means separating from the day-to-day "buddy" rela-tionships. Some distancing will occur automatically, assuming a new manager was promoted from the ranks of his peers. Those with whom he worked will see him differently and treat him differently by nature of the new authoritative position.

Help the new manager deal with the interpersonal relationship changes by giving him time to build new relationships with new peers–other managers and supervisors. Introduce him to people he can go to who are doing the same job he is. New managers need to gain the respect of their new management peers and get help from them.

Allow the new manager to establish new relationships by providing opportunities for him to associate with his management team outside of the work environment. Invite him to lunch or after-work gatherings where other managers participate. Hold management meetings where others in his position can be introduced to him. Be careful of after-work situations and do all you can to avoid appearances of impropriety.

One of the reasons the new manager was promoted to his position is most likely that he was good at what he did technically. He may be concerned about becoming stale and rusty in his chosen field if he does not stay current. Encourage him to remain technically up to date through reading publications and attending trade conferences. Suggest that he maintain his contacts in the group that he left in order to get updated information and occasionally bounce ideas off of those still involved with the hands-on, day-to-day technical issues.

Where the new supervisor once went to lunch with and socialized with his peers, he now has to establish new relationships with new colleagues. He now has to move from being friends with to being respected by those with whom he used to work.

"You will never find time for anything. If you want time you must make it."

— *Charles Buxton, English Author (1823-1871)*

"A positive attitude may not solve all your problems, but it will annoy enough people to make it worth the effort."

— *Herm Albright, Author (1876-1944)*

Striking a Work-Life Balance (In the Face of Increasing Demands)

Time management and organizational skills contribute to the leadership success of the people you promote. They need to establish practices that incorporate good time and organizational management so that the increased demands their leadership positions impose do not adversely affect their personal lives. Their people need to see them practice good time management and see that they can balance their work-life demands so that they, in turn, will be encouraged to do the same.

Managing time effectively and being organized help a manager be more productive on the job. She can keep the business in perspective with the rest of her life, which helps with making levelheaded decisions. Lower stress, which translates to less illness and fewer days off, can be the result of good time management and organizational practices. Exhibiting a model of efficiency and balance sets an example for employees to do the same, with similar benefits to them.

Encourage pursuing interests outside of work in order to allow people to step away from the job for awhile. They will return with better attitudes. Better relationship building within the organization may result from managers and employees pursuing broader interests and experiences related to non-work aspects of their lives. Self-esteem rises when a person defines herself and finds affirmation of her worth beyond the boundaries of her professional environment.

The higher a person climbs up the organizational ladder, the more demands are placed on her time. A *Fast Company* magazine Web interview by Linda Tischler with Catherine Hakim (sociology professor at the London School of Economics) reveals that "It takes prioritizing your career to the point where your private life, family life, and social life are wrapped around your career, rather than the two having equal weight. The key thing is not pre-plannable work, but the unexpected deadlines and crisis points that turn up at short notice. In practice, the higher up you go, by and large, jobs get greedier and greedier."[1] Restructuring the job to alter these demands is usually not possible. It is the nature of the game. This holds especially true for the new manager who is just learning about demands not yet known and trying to figure out how to balance the professional demands with the personal ones. The new manager can, however, structure her days, weeks and overall schedule to accommo-

---

[1] *http://www.fastcompany.com/articles/2004/01/hakim.html – The Best of Both Worlds.*

date the demands as well as devote time to other pursuits to create a more rounded life. Think about yourself and how you balance your own work-life demands. Ask yourself this question: "When I am ninety-five years old (God willing) and look back on my life, what will I wish I had done?" The answer is typically to spend more time with friends and family and to devote more of yourself to serving others. Seldom is it to have worked more. Unless you become personal friends with your colleagues, seldom will a former co-worker appear at your funeral. This may seem like a morbid point of view, but the question about what you will wish you had achieved is something I ask in my leadership workshops. It is a question you would do well to ask your new manager or supervisor, then help her create a process for establishing a schedule that contributes to her success in her new leadership position as well as her personal renewal outside of the job. She will be a better manager and better leader because of such a practice.

One key area that gets overlooked as demands increase is taking time for oneself. This does not have to mean taking a lot of time out for a vacation—though taking a week of vacation completely away from the work environment without taking work along is highly recommended at least once a year. (When I was a manager at "a large–blue–computer company" I would hear people brag that they had not taken a vacation in many years, accumulating days off that numbered in triple digits. I never understood this. While the work ethic is to be admired, the stress and strain on these people and their families had to have been incredible after a certain period of time.) Taking time for oneself does not have to mean taking a long time off from work. Self-care can be practiced at work during the day through work-rest choices. Cheryl Richardson, author of *Life Makeovers*, notes that working long hours at a frantic pace is counter-productive. Overwork and stress cause a variety of ills, including low creativity and stress-related illnesses that diminish effectiveness. Self-care tips include:

- Take lunch breaks and do something unrelated to work (walk, relax to personal music selections or write in a journal).

- Keep a consistent work schedule by arriving and leaving at approximately the same time each day—even if it is a ten- or twelve-hour workday.

- Learn to say no and don't take on more responsibility than can be handled—personally or by others.

A manager who practices self-care techniques encourages by example the people she influences.

Good time management practices include managing schedules to allow for efficiently handling correspondence (electronic, voice and hard copy) and direct contact with the people in the organization. Schedules also must allow for decision-making processes and contributing input to the business operations of concern with upper management. A new manager still needs time to complete her own staff work and personal responsibilities. For the work-life balance to be complete, she needs to take time for herself for renewal and rejuvenation outside of work, in addition to scheduling time for family, friends, faith and fun.

Meetings take up an inordinate percentage of time throughout the day. Advise new managers on how to conduct effective business meetings and to call or hold meetings only when necessary, involving only those people who need to be involved. Workshops, books and Web-based articles are available with articles, tips, forms and procedures on how to conduct efficient and effective business meetings (see "Resources" at the end of this chapter).

Time management and organizational skills can make or break a new manager. In addition to managing meetings, one must learn to delegate workload to others. Delegation requires empowering others to take responsibility and make decisions without micromanagement. Delegation requires strong communication skills to get messages across clearly and succinctly regarding expectations, conditions and implications. Trust must also be sustained between the two parties. Managing time sometimes means working smart rather than working hard. Not everything that needs to be done in a day really needs to be handled by the new manager. Tasks that do need to be attended to may be approached in a specific order that allows for multiple tasks being done at the same time or within close proximity of each other. Priorities should be determined so that important tasks are seen to before less important tasks. Whose priorities they are may determine how important they become! People, phone calls and impromptu electronic communications constantly interrupt a new manager. Managing interruptions so that the new manager's own duties are performed and responsibilities are met contributes to effective time management. Specific times of the day may need to be set for handling various types of interruptions. For example, an hour early in the morning, before most people arrive, may be allocated to handling electronic communications. The office door (or cubicle) may be open for a three-hour period every day to allow for people interruptions. Telephones can be rendered silent or calls sent directly to message services at specific times of the day, and then accumulated messages can be handled within another set time frame. Communication is the key to making efficient processes work. When others know explicitly when they can and cannot interrupt or how a person manages certain parts of a day, they tend to respect the parameters as well as business demands allow them to do so.

Organized work space and work processes also contribute to managing time and priorities throughout the day. The new supervisor should strive to handle paperwork and other communications one time only: Open it, read/listen to/watch it, decide where to store or how to handle it, do so, then move on. Work areas should have designated spaces for storing specific categories of information, data and reference material. Processes should be put into place so that work flows smoothly and so that others similarly affected by the workflow follow the processes. Stored information must be easily retrievable so that time is not wasted searching through scores of "stuff" trying to find what is needed. Computer equipment should be restricted to professional use—both as a means of minimizing the amount of information in the computer as well as setting an example for employee use of business equipment.

"Elegance of language may not be in the power of all of us; but simplicity and straightforwardness are. Write much as you would speak; speak as you think. If with your inferior, speak no coarser than usual; if with your superiors, no finer. Be what you say; and, within the rules of prudence, say what you are."

— King Alfred the Great (849, ruled England 871-899)

Communicate "Like Managers"

It is no secret that using effective communication skills results in having well-informed people. Information is empowerment, and an empowered workforce is a motivated and productive workforce. Responsibility for establishing and maintaining a strong communications channel within a department and across an organization starts with the management and leadership of the organization. People are better informed when their manager is a good communicator and the channels are in place for communicating. Employees are more likely to understand and then take ownership of their parts of the business. Management and leadership higher up in the organizational structure are better informed of the effects and consequences of their decisions and can react to the business climate experienced by the people in the trenches.

Managers and supervisors communicate a great deal of information. Some of what is communicated includes:

- Business climate → the state of the business and progress of the industry.
- Decisions → what and why they are made.
- Good news and bad.
- Vision, values, mission, goals and direction of the organization.
- Ideas and suggestions produced throughout the organization.
- Motivational messages.
- Policies, procedures and processes.
- Fun → encouraging an atmosphere that reflects humor and not taking oneself (and one's environment) too seriously.
- Infinite messages that influence and guide people and processes.

Communications channels that managers establish and in which they actively participate include their former co-workers, competitors (those who wanted the management position but did not get it) and colleagues (fellow managers). Channels also flow between supervisors and the people they supervise (direct reports and employees) as well as those who supervise the supervisor (from their own managers on up to the top of the organization chart). Customers and clients, key staff members other than direct reports, administrators and the supervisor's predecessors constitute other communications channels.

Continually practice effective communication skills, once learned or reinforced, in order to master them (if one can ever fully master communication skills). The anecdote has been told a thousand times about a man on a New York City street who hailed violinist Jascha Heifitz. The man asked Heifitz, "How do you get to Carnegie Hall?" to which Heifitz replied, "Practice!"

So, also, must presentation skills be practiced. One of the best ways to be visible to and noticed by people across an organization, especially for people in and striving for leadership positions, is to volunteer to give business presentations as often as possible. Stand in front of a group and lead a formal presentation and be viewed as the "go-to person" on the topic–even when the assumption is far from the truth. At many a presentation skills workshop, training session and Toastmasters International gathering, I have repeatedly heard it said that volunteering to give presentations, no matter how short or how long, is the fastest way to be noticed by other people and recognized as a candidate for leadership positions. It is also one of the most terrifying experiences for those who are not comfortable with presenting to more than two people at a time. It is a career-advisable step for a new manager to learn to give an effective business presentation.

To communicate well and present information, ideas and thoughts effectively, a leader must learn to listen. I have already mentioned the importance of strong listening skills earlier in this chapter. A quotation attributed to Oliver Wendell Holmes, Jr. (1841—1935) reads, "It is the province of knowledge to speak and it is the privilege of wisdom to listen." Leaders should demonstrate their wisdom.

If leadership is influence rather than authority, then the tool for influencing is communication. The new leader influences best by knowing how to organize thoughts, ideas and information and when to use specific persuasive techniques. Some of the most effective information-organization formats include:

- Whole-part-whole: presenting a concept in its entirety as a big picture, breaking the whole into parts with supporting points for each part and, finally, wrapping up by presenting the whole picture again (or from a complementary perspective).

- Chronological order: noting what comes first, second, third and so on along a time-related continuum.

- Cause/effect: communicating what causes a situation, then presenting the effects created by the situation on the business at hand.

- Problem/solution: stating a problem and following the problem statement with realistic solutions.

This last format is important for someone in a leadership position to adopt as a regular means of presenting situations that need to be solved. Advice given to me by my leadership mentors usually included the missive that if I were to bring up a problem that needed to be solved, I was to also suggest one or more solutions to the problem.

Leaders can influence by using positive words when they speak; for example, "can" rather than "can't" and "perhaps we will try that" instead of "it won't work." Another influential technique is to communicate how an action or decision will benefit the person affected by that action or decision. In other words, answer for them the question, "What's in it for me?" Mirroring a communication partner's style helps him or her relate better to what is being communicated. Understanding and using techniques that best reach people who communicate primarily within one or more communication styles (analytical, driver, expressive and amiable) opens communications channels that allow for greater influence with others.

Non-verbal signals also influence the message being communicated. Non-verbal signals include how one uses her voice (inflection, tone, speed, volume, vocal variety), what she does when communicating (looking away, making eye contact, leaning forward, standing at the doorway), and how she uses her body (gestures and facial expressions). A leader also needs to present an authoritative and respectful presence–commanding a room or situation just by the way she walks or speaks–in order to gain respect. This authoritative presence has little to do with gender, race, size or physical features. It is more an attitude of command and confidence that is communicated through good posture (sitting or standing), a strong handshake, direct eye contact, confident demeanor (even if not entirely felt) and assuring words spoken without hesitation or uncertainty. This attitude is what comes across as communicating "like a manager."

"Outstanding leaders go out of the way to boost the self-esteem of their personnel. If people believe in themselves, it's amazing what they can accomplish."

— *Sam Walton, Founder of the Wal-Mart Department Stores (1918-1992)*

Conclusion

Part of your responsibility for managing human resources–key resources to the bottom-line productivity and revenue of your business or organization–is to develop "people resources" to assume greater responsibilities. In this chapter, you received guidance to help you identify and develop the skills your new managers and supervisors need to succeed as leaders:

- Leadership skills that make a manager or supervisor a leader.
- Helping your new leader back away without turning off (staying technically current and maintaining relationships).
- Encouraging and supporting your managers in striking a work-life balance while facing increased demands.
- Skills that help your leaders communicate "like managers" with their people and with those higher up in their chain of command.

Help your management candidates and new supervisors develop these competencies that they will need in their leadership roles. A manager or supervisor who is recognized and respected as a leader will effectively move your organization's vision and goals through the people that he leads.

"Leadership is not so much about technique and methods as it is about opening the heart. Leadership is about inspiration–of oneself and of others. Great leadership is about human experiences, not processes. Leadership is not a formula or a program, it is a human activity that comes from the heart and considers the hearts of others. It is an attitude, not a routine."

— Lance Secretan, Author of "The New Story of Leadership: Moving to Higher Ground"

Management and Leadership Resources to Recommend

As part of your action plan to help new managers and supervisors learn to lead, consider referring them to the following resources.

Books, Publications and Media: Management and Leadership Development

- *Gung Ho! Turn on the People in Any Organization.* Ken Blanchard. William Morrow. ISBN #068815428X

- *Leader Effectiveness Training L.E.T.: The Proven People Skills for Today's Leaders Tomorrow.* Dr. Thomas Gordon. Perigree Publishing. ISBN #0399527133.

- *Principle-Centered Leadership.* Stephen Covey. Simon and Schuster. ISBN # 0671792806.

- Insight Publishing's *Power Learning: Real World Strategies* series → *Communication, Success, Leadership, Sales, Career Development, Customer Service, Management* and *Change.*

- Biographies of people you consider to be great leaders → of businesses, organizations, governments and people in general.

- HRLifeline.com → A Web resource with links to a gold mine of references, organizations and tools for managers and leaders (HR, management and leadership-related plus general references). This is a great time saver for finding a variety of legitimate, useful reference resources.

- ASTD *InfoLines* (<u>In</u>formation Life<u>lines</u>) → How-to and trends publications that are easy to read and filled with content–formatted as bullets, sidebars and reproducible worksheets. Each InfoLine is typically a sixteen-page 8.5" x 11" document that can be easily inserted into binders or notebooks. You do not have to be a member of ASTD (see below) to purchase these documents. http://www.astd.org/ASTD/Publications/infoline/. Topics include management development, business skills, career development, organizational development, performance and presentation skills.

Workshops and Training Programs

- American Management Association (AMA). www.AMAnet.org.
- American Society for Training and Development (ASTD). www.ASTD.org.
- Society for Human Resource Management (SHRM). www.SHRM.org.
- Franklin Covey Co. www.FranklinCovey.com.
- Springboard Training. www.SpringboardTraining.com.

Meetings

http://www.3m.com/meetingnetwork/

Work-Life Balance

Life Makeovers: 52 Practical & Inspiring Ways to Improve Your Life One Week at a Time. Cheryl Richardson. Broadway Publishing. ISBN #0767908848.

Communications Styles / Social Styles

People Styles at Work: Making Bad Relationships Good and Good Relationships Better. Robert Bolton and Dorothy Bolton. AMACOM Publishing. ISBN #0814477232.

About The Author

Sylvia Henderson

Sylvia Henderson conducts programs for organizations that want their people to communicate more clearly, lead more effectively, and be motivated to succeed personally and professionally. She facilitates workshops, develops educational tools, and is a published author of program-related articles. Programs range from keynotes to conference education sessions to facilitated workshops and training venues. She periodically conducts train-the-trainer sessions emphasizing classroom facilitation skills and creative visuals and presentation tools. Sylvia's programs highly involve her participants and include reference materials that reinforce learning beyond the programs. Her keynotes, best implemented as conference openers, set a motivating tone for an event and include take-aways so that the message is remembered. She weaves her avocation as a motorcyclist into messages that target her clients' needs. Sylvia's 20+ years with IBM and America Online include developing and delivering technical and human resource training. She was a team leader and manager practicing the leadership, communication and motivational skills she now presents in her programs. She holds an Education degree from Cheyney University (PA) and an MBA from the University of Pittsburgh (PA). She was accepted as a professional member of the National Speakers Association in 2001 and serves on the Boards of Directors of the DC Area chapter of NSA and the Girl Scout Council of the Nation's Capital.

Sylvia Henderson
Springboard Training
"Your springboard to personal and professional development!"
18005 Lafayette Drive – Suite B
Olney, MD 20832
Tel: 301-260-1538
Fax: (same – manual switchover)
Email: Sylvia@SpringboardTraining.com
www.SpringboardTraining.com